Crosscurrents/MODERN CRITIQUES

Crosscurrents/MODERN CRITIQUES

Harry T. Moore, *General Editor*

Contemporary
European Novelists

EDITED BY *Siegfried Mandel*

WITH A PREFACE BY
Harry T. Moore

SOUTHERN ILLINOIS UNIVERSITY PRESS
Carbondale and Edwardsville

FEFFER & SIMONS, INC.
London and Amsterdam

Preface

Contemporary European Novelists follows the volumes on today's American and British novelists in the Crosscurrents / Modern Critiques series. It is patterned somewhat differently, however, for instead of presenting a number of chapters on one or two novelists at a time, it takes entire literatures. This procedure, neatly fitting the present case, was determined by the editor of this volume, Professor Siegfried Mandel of the University of Colorado. He felt that a concentrated treatment of the novels of four nations would make possible a profounder approach than a wider survey. As a result, we have essays on the present-day fiction of Soviet Russia, France, Germany, and Italy.

European novels have become increasingly popular in the United States. Today we are so closely bound to Europe, so thoroughly acquainted with the Continent through news stories and television tours, that we want to know more about it and its people; and the novel is a compelling mode of discovery. But there is more in our interest than the merely utilitarian. Many of the problems of the people in those countries are our problems; reading about them brings us closer to them and expands our range of sympathy. The involvement a reader feels in a story gives him an emotional attachment to the subject matter; mere reports do not bring this condition about in a way that only the emotional-imaginative process of fiction can. Reading a novel, you participate in a special experience.

But perhaps the most salient point to consider is that many of these books are important literature. Hence they not only accomplish everything mentioned in the preceding paragraph, but they also provide the pleasure given by a work of art. They involve the highest sensibilities of man.

Most of the works discussed in the present volume are available in translation, for those who do not read the languages in which these books are originally written. But a number of them, as the authors of these essays note, have not yet been brought over into English; perhaps this book will induce publishers to engage translators for some of them and issue them over here.

The Soviet experience is particularly interesting to read about, for it has similarities to our own—particularly in the problems brought on by geographical vastness and what have been called power elites. Yet the Russian experience always has a magnetic alien touch. The Soviet writers are unfortunately often hobbled by censorship, but many of them deal rather fully with the collective life and its complications. Professor Deming Brown of the University of Michigan, who writes of Soviet literature in this volume, discusses the hampering effects of Stalinism on writers and points out that there has been partial relaxing in recent years (as, he also indicates, there was during the Second World War, when novels of front-line life became more humanized)—though, alas, at the time I am writing this, censorship seems to be tightening its grip again.

Mr. Brown sketches in his social background and then projects his discussions of individual writers against it. He tells us about novelists we know, providing some valuable insights into their work, and he also examines writers less familiar. As he indicates, although Tolstoy and Dostoevsky are still greatly admired by Russian writers, these newer men prefer short forms in their own work, the short story or the novella: "Their narrative scope more resembles that of Chekhov."

Poetry, as Mr. Brown says, has lately been the best part of Soviet literature; it can be nebulous in a way that novels, forced to adhere to socialist realism, cannot be; hence the poems have fewer limitations and are less liable to censorship. There is no Russian Camus, and Camus's works are unavailable in Russia. Mr. Brown cites Sinyavsky's statement to the effect that Soviet literature will grow when its writers are permitted to turn to the fantastic and the absurd. Perhaps it is a hopeful sign that Mikhail Bugalov, who died in 1940, was "rehabilitated" in 1966; his novel of the absurd and the grotesque, The Master and Margarita, was published in Russia and abroad.

Professor Wallace Fowlie of Duke University writes of the French novel in the present book. Professor Fowlie has written on this subject before, but here he brings it up to date and offers important new perspectives. He begins with the existentialists and shows how many varied concerns their novels have. He also points out the continuity of self-revelation in the French novel, from La Princess de Clèves in the seventeenth century on through to the works of Marcel Proust and Jean Genet in the twentieth. Mr. Fowlie deals rather thoroughly with Genet, whom he has not treated at such length in earlier writings; likewise the "anti-novel" school receives more space here than Mr. Fowlie has given it before. His remarks about Nathalie Sarruate, Alain Robbe-Grillet, Michel Butor, and others among the newer writers are highly illuminating. And he writes with particular eagerness about G. M. G. Le Clézio, whose merits both Mr. Fowlie and Henri Peyre have been pointing out to American readers in the last year or so. Mr. Fowlie closes his lively essay by pointing out that the hero of today's French novels is no longer the committed man, the existentialist, but a new type of protagonist, "nondescript" but none the less interesting as he acts out his chaotic destiny.

Professor Mandel, who has written an entire volume for Crosscurrents / Modern Critiques (Rainer Maria Rilke: The Poetic Instinct), deals in the present book with the contemporary German novel. He begins by discussing the destructive legacy the Nazi years left to

German literature, which had to make a new beginning after 1945. Mr. Mandel shows the poets, dramatists, and novelists finding themselves amid the dust of ruins and going on to create a new literature. Mr. Mandel is particularly good on the subject of Heinrich Böll and his "major novel," Billiards at Half-Past Nine, that family story crossing three generations. Mr. Mandel refuses to see much likeness between Böll and Gerd Gaiser, who have often been compared; Mr. Mandel admires Gaiser's skill, but dislikes his ideological tendencies. Mr. Mandel gives an interesting explication of the work of the rather difficult Uwe Johnson, and he sees Günter Grass as an exuberant satirist in the great tradition of François Rabelais and Laurence Sterne. But Mr. Mandel is cautious about making any predictions in relation to the German novel of the future; there is still widespread disillusionment, and there are such irritating problems as the Berlin Wall: "The new generation has inherited unenviable legacies. How these are dealt with, the newer novelists will let us know."

Professor Louis Tenenbaum, chairman of the Department of Italian at Colorado, points out, in his discussion of the Italian novel, that the novel itself is a comparatively new art form in Italy. Yet Italian fiction today is rich in variety and often deep, though the Italian writers, like their counterparts in Germany, are often haunted by the recent Fascist past.

Mr. Tenenbaum examines that past and shows how the the regime failed to get an official literature established. The finest writers in the 1930's associated themselves with two literary reviews, Solaria and its successor, Letteratura, whose names are "suggestive of the renewed approach by Italian writers to the problem of literary expression in fiction, an approach which brought Europe, America, and the neglected writers of Italy's own recent past together to enliven contemporary Italian writing."

In subsequent passages, Mr. Tenenbaum deals with

Albert Moravia, Elio Vittorini, Vasco Pratolini, Cesare Pavese, and others who helped create the newer literature. He brings his account up to date by examining Carlo Emilio Gadda and other more recent writers, always providing a vital discussion of their works and relating them to trends.

Written exclusively for this book, these four essays on the European novel of today give us an unusually full picture of that medium as it stands in its place and time, and it further provides us with significant discussions of the important individual novelists as they appear against those backgrounds.

HARRY T. MOORE

Southern Illinois University
May 11, 1968

Notes on Contributors

DEMING BROWN is the author of *Soviet Attitudes toward American Writing, A Guide to Soviet Russian Translations of American Literature,* and several articles on Soviet Russian literature. Currently, he is writing a book on Russian literature since the death of Stalin. He is Professor of Russian Literature in the Department of Slavic Languages and Literatures at the University of Michigan.

WALLACE FOWLIE is the author of *The French Critic,* appearing in the Crosscurrents Series, as well as author of books on Rimbaud, Gide, Mallarmé, Proust, Cocteau, and Claudel. He contributes regularly to literary and scholarly journals. He has translated numerous poetic and dramatic works — classical and modern — from the French and is James B. Duke Professor of French at Duke University.

SIEGFRIED MANDEL is the author of *Rainer Maria Rilke: The Poetic Instinct,* which appeared in the Crosscurrents Series. He has edited and introduced the volume *Rainer Maria Rilke: Visions of Christ.* He has contributed articles, reviews, and features to leading periodicals. Presently he teaches English and is Professor of Comparative Literature at the University of Colorado.

LOUIS TENENBAUM has published articles and reviews principally in the field of modern Italian fiction, contributing to such journals as the *Bucknell Review, Cesare Barbieri Courier, Modern Language Quarterly,* and *Symposium.* He is Chairman of the Department of Italian at the University of Colorado and is currently engaged in a study of the Italian writer and World War I.

Contents

Introduction

In this companion volume to *Contemporary American Novelists* and *Contemporary British Novelists*, we had to choose between horizontal coverage of the European novel, across all countries producing fiction, or to narrow our scope to a greater in-depth treatment of fiction in those countries whose novelists are most influential today and who have gained international attention. We chose the latter course. Each contributor was asked to evaluate, criticize, and explain freely novels and authors within his own area of familiarity, as well as to render the intellectual and political contexts and trends that have shaped French, German, Italian, and Russian postwar fiction. Readers of the original essays included in *Contemporary European Novelists* will find that the authors also have drawn upon some sources of criticism and fiction still untranslated, but which merit translation, in order to give an organic focus to the careers of the writers discussed.

In searching for answers as to what gives contemporary European literature its distinct features, one particularly notices the surge of experimentation and technical variations, the writers' painful and often orphaned isolation—despite ideological groupings—and their awareness of it as a source of creativity and frustration, as well as their essential combativeness. Writing down his thoughts about the relationship of artistic productivity and social development, while incarcerated during the time of Italian totalitarianism, Antonio Gramsci observed: "Opposed to the uprightness and spontaneity of literature and art is a false conformism, a false communality, and a people suiting themselves to handy ideas which have become stale through custom." Whatever is false in conformism, communality, and custom has become indeed the target of the novelists' censure. A kind of heady incaution—though at a considerable risk to the Russian fiction writers—quickens the art of European novelists. Art is nourished by their opposition and opposition is nourished by their art. As a result, the tensions which have been generated among artists, critics, audience, and the political powers have revived some of the literary excitement stirred by "modernism" in the arts earlier in the century. Dependence upon tradition has weakened—especially in those countries where totalitarianism had and has disoriented cultural life—and a spirit of individualism has set in, a spirit essential to meaningful literature. By the same token, there are divisions of outlook—political, philosophical, esthetic—among writers; some seek their goal through affirmation while others seek it through negation. But whatever their philosophy, through literature it has gained greater power than it had as philosophy. Existentialism is a case in point.

Links with pan-European literary traditions and with American writings have been reforged in a small measure, with minimal effect in Russian literature, but more important is the attempt by novelists to have their work reach out beyond national boundaries and to establish contact with other peoples. Much of what has been written has aspects of universality—the common, relevant themes which touch every human heart and mind, despite the differing and changing settings, though these too hold particular fascination for readers who wish to understand the so-called national character of a country and its life. Little has been said in our essays about comparative "influences"; the feeling seems to be that though they are operative, they are not quite assimilated to native soils.

Many of the leading European novelists have travelled extensively and have gained an objectivity about their immediate world, which is reflected in their works. This objectivity is evident in overt or implied criticism and in awareness of social conditions to the point of sharp detail, at times excessive, and through a passion for documentation, which often verges on the journalistic. Their documentation has a sociological base and permits a thorough and confident scrutiny of life as it is, and rarely, as in idealistic literature, what it might be. The approach has encouraged a preference for the I-narrator who can get as close as possible to life. However, the introspective approach has not been neglected for externals. Much of the literature is defined by psychological realism, introspective and confessional, with streaks of satire. If the Russian novelists seem to ignore the Freudian sphere, the others do not; while the French open every private area of action and thought to observation, the German novelists do not compete with erotic imports, particularly from America.

One of the signal services the new literature has performed is the rummaging of the spiritual ruins of the past and stripping away lingering facades that obscure some ugly truths. Their warnings point to the future. We find then among European writers a literature of participation and engagement, often at the expense of personal safety and in the face of harassment, which speaks not only of the debasement of man but also of his dignity.

SIEGFRIED MANDEL

Boulder, Colorado
February 5, 1968

Contemporary European Novelists

Soviet Russian Fiction
Changes, Challenges, and Frozen Propositions

DEMING BROWN

Soviet Russian literature has resumed its candid exploration of human affairs. It has begun to restate propositions that are taken for granted in the literature of the West: the uniqueness of the individual personality; the right of the conscience to question institutionalized sets of morals and ethics; the dignity of introspection, of private thoughts and tastes; the recognition of a common humanity in art, independent of political and social systems.

In the early 1950's, Soviet literature had approached a state of moribundity. It was policed by an elaborate and thorough-going censorship and burdened with officially-prescribed didactic functions. It was constricted by a narrow conception of human nature, human affairs, and historical processes. And it was governed, ultimately, by the caprice of the world's most powerful dictator. A few novelists, such as Victor Nekrasov, Vera Panova, and the veterans Konstantin Fedin, Leonid Leonov, and Konstantin Paustovsky, had managed to preserve something of the traditional depth and sensitivity of Russian fiction; and others, such as Boris Pasternak, preserved their values by writing in private. For the most part, however, writers, in order to be published at all, had been forced to become dishonest, or superficial, or both.

Political expediency and the mandate of official optimism forbade the mention of large areas of social evil; others were glossed over as incidental terrain, crossed in the inevitable march of progress. The result was a mass literature of social and emotional make-believe, under the guise of "socialist realism." As reading matter it was dull, unimaginative, and predictable. The heritage of Stalinism still dominates much of Soviet literature today, but in the past fifteen years much has been done to undermine it. For one thing, satire—which was formerly restricted to the "constructive" purpose of assisting the regime in castigating its enemies—has been granted a wider latitude. Here is a passage from "Two Comrades," a story by Vladimir Voinovich, published in 1967:

> Our city was divided into two parts—the old one, where we lived, and the new one, where we didn't live. The new one was usually called "beyond the Palace," because in the vacant land between the old part and the new one they were building this Palace, the biggest, as we said, in the country. At first it was supposed to be the biggest Palace of metallurgists in the country, in the style of Corbusier. The Palace was almost finished when it was ascertained that the author of the plans had been subjected to the influence of Western architecture. They soaped his neck for that Corbusier so much that he was a long time in coming to. Then came new times, and they let the author return to his interrupted work. But now he was no fool and, just in case, he appended to the building some hexahedral columns, standing off to the side. The construction began to be called the Palace of science and technology, also the biggest in the country. After the installation of the columns, they again bottled up the construction; under the biggest Palace in the country they found the biggest underground spring. Several more years passed—what became of the water I don't know—they resumed construction, but now this had become the biggest Palace of weddings in Europe.[1]

The ironical and irreverent tone of this passage would have been impossible fifteen years ago. Its highly sarcastic evocation of the history of Soviet architecture—and, by implication, of the Soviet arts in general—its ridicule of ham-handed administrative bullying and bungling, and its humorous reflection of Soviet mores (it doesn't matter whether the Palace is used for metallurgists or weddings, it's still the biggest something-or-other), all strike a note that was long absent from Soviet letters. Such a passage recalls the iconoclasm of Ilya Ilf and Evgeny Petrov, a team of humorists of the nineteen-thirties whose works were under an official cloud for nearly twenty years until they were republished in the middle fifties.

Although opportunities for literary expression have been gradually expanding, Soviet writers still want much more freedom, and their creative efforts would be a great deal bolder and more experimental if they were permitted it. The rules are still set and administered by political authorities: the censorship still operates. The directors of publishing houses and the editors of magazines are still subject to centralized Party discipline. Opportunities for contact with foreign literature are still limited by controls over the translation or importation of literature from abroad. The freedom to question and to shake up preconceptions, to startle, to disturb, and to mystify, is still limited. A prudish antiscepticism prevents the full exploration of dark sides of human nature; social alienation can be sympathetically described only at great peril.

An indication of the limits beyond which Soviet prose writers cannot step is provided in the works of Andrei Sinyavsky, who sent manuscripts abroad after despairing of seeing them published in the Soviet Union, and who suffered severely for doing so. Sinyavsky's short novels *The Trial Begins* and *Lyubimov* (translated as *The Make-peace Experiment*) and his *Fantastic Stories*[2] are loaded with grotesque and savage satire, singling out situations of corruption and social injustice in naturalistic detail. Collectively they suggest a society in the grip of sweeping moral sickness, dominated by a class of brutes and hypocrites. Sinyavsky displays, in addition, a sexual candor and an interest in unconscious drives that would probably have scared off even the most daring of Soviet editors. His use of hyperbole, symbolism, and the fantastic often verges on surrealism. These devices, applied ironically to a clearly identifiable Soviet social context, can easily (although, I think, unfairly) be construed as being maliciously and destructively critical—and they were so construed by the court which in 1966 sentenced Sinyavsky to seven years at hard labor.[3] Even had Sinyavsky's fiction been devoid of immediate political import, it is doubtful whether it would have been accepted for publication. For Soviet editors still have little tolerance for the ambiguous, the grotesque, or the bizarre. The governing principle of Soviet literature is still socialist realism, with emphasis on the pursuit of demonstrable, functional truth through direct and lucid means.

Although clarity and comprehensibility are still *sine qua non*, recently the range and depth of permissible inquiry have been increased, to permit a more comprehensive and elastic understanding and a more subtle and resonant expression of "truth." Socialist realism, with its obligation to affirm, indoctrinate, educate, and reassure, has begun to give ground to critical realism, with its freedom to question, evaluate, and negate. It is still impossible for Soviet commentators to admit frankly that this transition is taking place. Socialist realism is still the only officially-recognized literary credo. Critics and theoreticians who have recently suggested that there is now room for *two* "realisms" have been firmly reminded that this would require a major ideological revision by the central cultural authorities and that such a decision is not about to be made. Nevertheless, many writers—including all of the best ones—seem to be ignoring this fact, and there is now evident in Soviet literature an enormous lag between officially proclaimed theory and actual practice. And although the practice of critical realism lacks a recognized ideological underpinning, it does have a kind of official sanction stemming from the decision of the Twentieth Congress of the Communist Party in 1956 to expose what is euphemistically called the "cult of personality" of Stalin. This exposure, in which the literary community has eagerly participated, has involved both a re-examination of the past and a re-evaluation of the present.

By the early 1950's, the writing community had developed an enormous frustration and sense of collective guilt for having participated, for more than a quarter-century, in the systematic suppression and distortion of the facts of Soviet life and for having rationalized and prettified the injustice, inhumanity, and betrayal of ideals that were characteristic of Stalin's times. A major feature of the writing of recent years has been its effort to settle accounts with the past, to correct the record, and to atone, insofar as possible, for the failure of literature to act as the conscience of the nation during its years of most extreme corruption and suffering. It is a process that involves both a feeling of civic duty and a recognition of the necessity of cultural —specifically esthetic—rehabilitation. Indeed, writers realize that unless a national literature cultivates the habit of honesty and develops the freedom to pursue its goals with integrity—whatever these goals may be —it cannot achieve esthetic fulfillment.

Although writers are not free to deal with all aspects of the Stalinist past, they have been officially encouraged, in the interest of exposing the "cult of personality," to treat many of its features with considerable candor. They are not as free to be frank in writing about the contemporary scene. It is therefore safer to write about evils that have, presumably, been overcome than to write about those which are manifestly still thriving. The exploration of the past, however, has a peculiar relevance for the present, for despite important transformations in the quality of Soviet life, the residue of Stalinist times remains prominent. As a result, there has arisen a kind of unspoken convention through which writers feature situations and moral problems in past settings which have obvious but tacit counterparts and parallels in the present. Under such terms they can deal with the present—at one remove —with relative impunity. Much of Soviet prose is not as retrospective as it seems to be on the surface.

Pavel Nilin's novel *Cruelty* (translated as *Comrade Venka*) first published in 1956, is a good example of moral re-evaluation of the past that has a contemporary—in fact a timeless—relevance. The story, set in Siberia in the days of the Civil War that followed the October Revolution, recounts events leading up to the suicide of Venka Malishev, a young Cheka (secret police) officer. Assigned the job of investigating a band of counterrevolutionary guerillas, Venka develops a sympathy for, and wins the confidence of, one of their leaders. Through careful persuasion, Venka brings his man to the verge of political rehabilitation and induces him to turn himself in. Venka's world is shattered when his superior officer callously betrays him by entrapping and arresting his man as a common political criminal. A problem of political morality, of simple human decency, compassion, and honor as opposed to revolutionary expediency, is raised in this novel to the level of genuine tragedy. There is no affirmation here of the moral rightness of historical processes: an intelligent, idealistic young man is crushed to the point of self-destruction by the realization that he has been the instrument of an evil trick performed in what he has believed to be the cause of social justice. With its sharp focus on a single moral issue—the issue of ends and means—the novel, although set in what is now a remote period, resounds to the present, unpoisoned by the false optimism and specious justifications that are typical of the literature of socialist realism.

The collectivization of agriculture which took place

in the early 1930's has long been the subject of works of fiction. The class tensions and bloody conflicts involved in the dispossession of millions of private peasants were a source of tremendous drama. At the same time writers have traditionally been obligated to justify this epoch of suffering and deprivation by emphasizing its benefits: the rationalization of agriculture, the positive transformation in human relationships, and the development of a new constructive socialist spirit in the countryside. Evil in such works was identified with a greedy counterrevolutionary hankering for private ownership and a selfish, individualistic preference for managing one's own affairs independently. The typical central figure of such works was a dedicated, practical, self-denying organizer, a communist activist motivated by a dream of collective abundance and social justice. Mikhail Sholokhov's *Virgin Soil Upturned* has long been the most prominent novel on this theme.

A retrospective novel on the theme of collectivization is Sergei Zalygin's *On the Irtysh,* published in 1964.[4] It is the story of the destruction of a natural leader, the strongest and wisest man in his Siberian community. He is willing to join the newly-formed collective, but he refuses to risk starvation for his family by contributing his last ounce of wheat to the common store of seed-grain. His very qualities of uprightness, self-reliance, and a firm sense of personal responsibility—qualities badly needed in the building of the new order—are precisely the ones that antagonize the regional organizers, who insist on his blind acceptance of official decrees. Ultimately it is a simple, decent act of compassion that brings about his downfall: he shelters the innocent wife and children of a saboteur in defiance of his ignorant and terrorized neighbors. Badgered and cheated by the local authorities, alienated from his confused and suspicious fellow-peasants, he is dispossesed, ripped from his community, and exiled.

Potentially the most poignant theme of retrospective literature are the concentration camps, which were the ugliest feature of the Stalinist regime and the most vivid symbol of the horrors of the police state. Although many recent works have mentioned the camps by indirection or in passing, only one story with a camp setting has been allowed publication. Alexander Solzhenitsyn's *One Day in the Life of Ivan Denisovich* is the chronicle, from reveille to lights out, of an ordinary day in the ten-year imprisonment of a simple peasant who has been unjustly and arbitrarily convicted of treason. Solzhenitsyn creates, with intense compression, a complex, self-contained world that can be taken as a microcosm of the betrayed, beaten, morally devastated nation of which it was a product. At the same time, in the person of his hero and numerous fellow-prisoners, Solzhenitsyn made a testament of the endurance of the human spirit in the face of inhuman physical deprivation, insult, and spiritual torture. The novel is not merely a social document, but a literary masterpiece, and although it deals with an institution with which millions of Russians were already familiar—either through personal experience or word of mouth—its quiet authenticity, multitude of evocative characters, and spiritual profundity have caused its publication to be regarded by many Russians as the greatest single event in the literature of recent times.

The quantity of Soviet prose fiction about World War II is enormous. During the war itself, fiction was of course intensely patriotic and hortatory, but it was also humane. Considerations of ideology and indoctrination in correct attitudes toward service to the state and society were subordinated to compassionate and proud depictions of suffering, courage, and endurance. Some of the finest works about the war—notably Vera Panova's *Traveling Companions* (translated as *The Train*) and Victor Nekrasov's *In the Trenches of Stalingrad* (translated as *Front-Line Stalingrad*)—appearing within a year of its close, are notable for their close and loving attention to individual character, to private motivations, and to intimate feelings. Very shortly after the war, however, the literature concerning it became, in response to official pressures, intensely political and chauvinistic. The function of war fiction became one of demonstrating the role of Communist Party leadership and ideology in mobilizing the victory over Hitler's armies, of showing the indispensability of Stalin's leadership, and of proving that the heroic exploits that won the war could only have been accomplished by the especially endowed New Soviet Man.

In contrast to the latter type of war fiction, the literature that has appeared since 1956 has reasserted, and even expanded upon, the humane quality of that which was written during the war. It has indeed had a political function: to show the military unpreparedness—now attributed to Stalin's bungling and his mass purges of Red Army officers—that permitted the initial rapid German advances deep into Russia; to demonstrate how Stalin's cruelty, rigidity, and suspiciousness crippled the war effort by causing needless sacrifices of human life and resources; and to illustrate numerous other corrections of the military record. But most of all, recent war fiction has emphasized the individual human experience and its significance: the moral problems involved in command decisions; the effects of the fear and sight of death, and the loss of comrades, on the human psyche; the nature of a sense of duty, of loneliness, of self-reliance, and of bravery. In the pursuit of these interests, the latest military fiction has become somewhat less heroic and has dwelt on the sheer, intrinsic ghastliness of war and its senseless, nightmarish qualities. In the hands of such writers as Yuri Bondarev, Vladimir Bogomolov, Vasily Bykov, and Bulat Okudzhava, it has begun to display a pacifistic strain reminiscent of Erich Remarque and Hemingway—a strain quite uncharacteristic of the writing that appeared during the war and the decade immediately following.

The resurgence of the theme of World War II at a time when Western writers had already exhausted and abandoned it was of course a response to new opportunities for truth-telling. The chance to write afresh about the war and to deal with its human implications with new sensitivity and candor also permitted writers to use the conflict as leverage for an evaluation of the more recent past—and, by implication, the present. Many stories and novels employ a time-span that enables them to embrace both the war and the period up to the death of Stalin (or thereabouts). Such works usually draw a contrast between front-line morality, where individual honesty, loyalty, and cooperation among comrades are indispensable, and where the single purpose of destroying a monolithic enemy brings about a pragmatic knowledge of right and wrong, and a complex and corrupt peacetime scene, where falsity and moral compromise are a prominent feature of life. Yuri Bondarev has written two novels on this theme. In *Silence*, Sergei Vokhmintsev, a demobilized young army captain who is now a student at a mining institute, meets up in a Moscow cafe with Uvarov, another former officer whom Sergei alone knows to have been guilty of front-line cowardice that cost the lives of several comrades. Enraged at the sight of Uvarov, Sergei beats him up. In the course of the novel, through intrigue in Communist Party circles and with the fortuitous help of a secret-police frameup that sends Sergei's father to a concentration camp, Uvarov succeeds in engineering Sergei's expulsion from both the Party and the institute. The novel stresses the loneliness, isolation, and frustration of a young man whose wartime habits of stubborn honesty and direct confrontation of injustice do not seem applicable in a peacetime world of secret denunciations, careerism and double cross. In Bondarev's related novel *The Two*,[5] Sergei's friend Kostya, also a veteran who is now a Moscow taxi-driver, keeps a Luger—awarded to him as a souvenir at the front for bravery—as protection against thugs who prey upon taxi-drivers at night. It is illegal for him to have the gun: the state, which he risked his life to defend against outside enemies, cannot now protect him against enemies within; nevertheless he has been ordered to turn in his arms. Symbolically, Kostya throws his gun into a canal shortly after he learns of the death of Stalin.

In their exposure of Stalinist ideology, writers now sometimes uncover soft spots in the system of belief that has survived Stalin. In Vladimir Tendryakov's *A Rendezvous with Nefertiti,* published in 1965, there is a discussion among four war veterans, all of them art students, who have just participated in a demonstration on Red Square over which Stalin, like a deity, has presided. One of the young men argues that Stalinism is a religion, necessary for the preservation of a sense of national purpose and order. Another, who believes completely in Stalin and everything he stands for, nevertheless maintains that Stalinism cannot be a religion because Stalin himself is mortal. As it develops, however, the whole dispute turns on the question of sacrifice in the name of future generations and one's willingness to suspend moral judgments for the sake of attaining communist goals.

> [You say] forget yourself completely, live for your great grandson. Can a man really live only for mirages of the future? There is an oppressive injustice in this— you are fertilizer! The heralds of a marvelous future,— what right do they have to treat one with such scornful arrogance?
>
> .　.　.　.　.　.　.　.　.　.　.　.　.
>
> In order to have blind faith, I must have confirmation. The idea must manifest itself every day before I'll begin to be convinced that blood is flowing less and less, —and it must manifest itself now, and not after my death. Why must I believe blindly? [6]

The burden of this discussion is clearly to refute the "cult of personality." Yet it is curiously reminiscent of the arguments of Ivan Karamazov against the existence of God and of Yuri Zhivago's statement that "man is born to live, not to prepare for life." Its polemic thrust can easily extend, although this may not have been the author's conscious intention, to the heart of communist belief in the inevitability of historical progress.

It is significant that the discussion quoted takes place among art students, for a vast quantity of the literature of recent years is devoted to problems of creativity, artists, and the arts. Conscious of having passed through a long period of creative drought, writers have been combing over this aspect of the past with almost masochistic thoroughness. In novel after novel, a painter, poet, or inventor—almost invariably a veteran who has proved his manhood and patriotic devotion at the front—struggles to find self-expression in the stifling, frustrating atmosphere of Stalin's Russia, which is dominated by an establishment of officially-approved hacks who have prostituted their talents. Such novels usually have happy endings: Stalin passes from the scene, and after years of heartbreaking discouragement the hero gets his opportunity to contribute his gifts to society. However, this socialist-realist ingredient—the happy ending—does not in itself vitiate the substance of such works, and it is not always present. What is important in these novels is their meticulous exposure of the falsity, shallow pretentiousness, and time-serving quality of the officially-inspired art and literature that formerly prevailed and that still, though threatened, appears to have a long lease on life. Novels devoted to such themes abound not only in earnest dialogues about the nature and purpose of art but also in parodies of opportunistic writing and ironic descriptions of socialist-realist art. An example of the latter is in A Rendezvous with Nefertiti, in which the hero, who has just graduated from an art institute and is hungry for work, is offered a commission to do a painting to decorate a wall in a new Moscow hotel. To give the young artist an idea of

what he wants, the hotel director shows him a photo-
graph of a typical socialist-realist painting:

> . . . under the open sky long tables, heaped with food,
> roast goose, hillocks of apples, around the tables the
> beards of venerable old men, the neckties of young
> ones, embroidered Russian blouses, girls' dresses in the
> city style. A reproduction of the familiar . . . "Collec-
> tive Farm Wedding."
>
> "Create for us something like this picture. With all
> the, so to say, optimism and life-affirming quality of this
> work . . . a gala holiday in our Soviet countryside,
> sunny, joyful. In a word, in the spirit of this same work,
> but in your own style, so that it will be an independent
> work . . . One meter eighty centimeters by two meters
> twenty five centimeters." [7]

Although he is virtually starving, the hero flatly refuses
this fat commission.

Paintings in the spirit of the one described above
can now be derided in print with a degree of impunity,
since they were indeed a feature of Stalinist times. But
not as much has been changed as might have been
changed. Such paintings still enjoy official favor, and
they continue to be produced in great abundance. And
in many other respects there is an essential similarity
between the Soviet past and the present. In fostering a
carefully controlled revelation of the past, Soviet authorities are anxious to prevent a public dwelling on
and brooding about evils that have still not been eradi-
cated. Also, they are anxious to avoid the public indignation that might result from a too frank and thorough examination of institutions—such as the secret
police and concentration camps—for which many persons still in positions of power and authority were
responsible. Writers are therefore urged to push
ahead, to concern themselves with the problems of the
present and the promise of the future, in the hope that
after a number of years a cushion of remoteness will
enable the writing community to deal with past evils
without excessively depressing public morale.

From the foregoing it is evident that contemporary Soviet literature, taken as a whole, aspires to provide a direct and accurate reflection of the objective world— that is, it tries to stay "close to life." The reasons are partly traditional—even socialist realism pretends to value this quality above all others. But the present-day concern over facts and objective truth is also the expression of a deeply-felt need to restore the veracity of Russian literature. As a critic has recently said, "people avidly want the truth and are on their guard against half-truth." [8] There is accordingly a tendency, even among fully-committed writers of fiction, to mistrust their own fantasy and to bolster up and justify their own inventions with large quantities of documentary material, to "place their confidence in reality." Both the contemporary short story and the novel tend to be heavily infused with such authenticating data. And nearly every prominent writer of fiction also engages in journalism, the writing of travel essays, memoirs, and local-color sketches that describe the country in detail—its physical environment, its activities, and its people. Many prose writers—among them Valentin Ovechkin, Efim Dorosh, Gavriil Troepolski, Vladimir Soloukhin, and Olga Berggol'ts (the last two are also accomplished poets)—have established distinguished reputations through the cultivation of this *genre*, which in Russia today is considered esthetically as important as fiction. Through the medium of documentary and semi-documentary prose a large sociological study seems to be taking place. Its greatest current success is its investigation, often sharply critical, of life on the collective farms, by such writers as Dorosh and Fyodor Abramov. On this theme, as on many others, as a Soviet critic has pointed out, many Russian writers seem currently to be replacing "the hero felt" with "I saw this." [9]

In fiction the search for veracity through the amassing of directly-observed detail has begun to produce an increasingly inclusive and many-sided examination of social environment. An example of the new objectivity is Vitaly Syomin's novel *Seven in One House*, published in 1965. The novel is set in a neglected suburb of a large Soviet city (probably Rostov-on-Don), where, because of the chronic housing shortage, families are jammed together in close quarters. The essence of the novel is not, however, its depiction of crowded housing (this is already a convention in Soviet literature), but its dispassionate portrayal (suggestive of Alan Sillitoe) of ordinary working-class Soviet citizens engaged in the business of daily living. A goodly proportion of them are shown to be as petty, selfish, unambitious, and indolent as the usual run of humans everywhere. Concerned with their own mundane affairs, they seem totally uninterested in ideology and devoid of the sense of lofty purpose and direction which Soviet citizens are traditionally supposed to feel. They work as much as they have to, they produce children, they gossip, they drink and occasionally brawl (an accidental murder takes place in the course of a senseless street-fight). They are closely tied to, and bound by, a drab environment.

The central figure in the novel is Mulya Konyukhova, a middle-aged war widow who has managed to shelter simultaneously in her small, dilapidated house, four generations of her family, including her stupid, eccentric mother and her dull, lazy, and generally worthless son. Although Mulya's life has been one of heroic sacrifice (during the war and for several years after she had only one dress, and nearly starved to feed her family), the author has been careful not to give her a saintly coloration. She is garrulous and earthy; she despises her mother and has coddled and spoiled her son. But her chief qualities are an ingrained sense of responsibility and a spunky independence. Here is part of her account of her job in a shoe factory:

> We took on socialist obligations—we were competing with a shoe factory in another region. Well, and how did they take on these socialist obligations? They made

the arrangements somewhere in the director's office or Party factory committee, and brought them to us in the shop to vote on. "Who's 'for'? Who's 'against?' Nobody?" I say, "I'm against." They didn't even believe me, they thought they must have heard me wrong: "Is there anyone against?" I say, "I'm against. You've got it written there that you're going to lower the cost-price and increase labor productivity by twenty-five percent . . . But how to increase it? We don't have machines. We have manual labor. How are you going to increase productivity? By speeding up manual labor? You write: 'Insure by mechanization a hundred-percent increase in labor productivity'—and I'm to agree to a hundred percent." They yell at me: "You're not our kind of person!"—"It's you," I say, "who are not our kind of people." Next day they call me up before the factory committee: "You said that the communists of the factory are not our kind of people?"—"And you are communists?"—I ask. "Watch your words, Konyukhova! You're lucky it's not the old days. We'll take educational measures with you."

And what kind of educational measures do they take with me? They move me from a high piece-work rate to a low one. They'll turn everybody against me. But you see, I'm so fast. I work very fast. My organism is like that. I work as much as two young people. How can there be equality in manual labor? You are healthy, you are quick—for you one norm, for a weak person another. They put me to riveting straps—and in one shift I make twice as big a heap of them as anybody else. . . . The women get peeved at me, but I tell them: "Why did you vote for that agreement? I voted against it! And you're mad because the quotas are killing you."

The bosses don't like me. They don't like me, but they can't do anything about it—they can't give me a worse job because there isn't any, and I always overfulfill the plan. . . .[10]

Mulya's dialogue continues with a complaint about the factory director, who is harsh and rude to the workers, who cares only about increasing production, and who refuses to replace broken windows that cause nasty draughts in the shop. What is significant about this passage, however, is not its criticism of factory mismanagement and working conditions (this has always been permissible, to a degree, in Soviet literature), but the fact that the system of socialist incentives—long a major factor in Soviet industry—can be attacked with such candor. Even more significant is the fact that the *working* career of Mulya plays such a small, incidental role in the total narrative. Mulya is, after all, a very good factory worker, yet the author's treatment of this aspect of her life is confined to the brief passage just cited.

Mulya works because she is in the business of earning a living. She works well because she is naturally quick and energetic, and not because of an awareness that the purpose of her labor is to build communism. Like Mulya, increasing numbers of major characters in Soviet fiction who take pride in their occupational skills nevertheless do not endow their competence with ideological significance. Work is just one of the things everybody does, and there is no particular reason to get excited about it.

This is a far cry from the notions that predominate in the traditional Soviet production novel, in which characters are measured in terms of their attitudes toward the enterprise in which they are employed, and in which enthusiasm for the job springs from being infected with the collective spirit. The central situation of a typical production novel is a work-site, a large industrial enterprise, which is either in the process of being built or is engaged in a drive to increase production. An essential ingredient of such novels is one or more "positive heroes," leaders whose example of zeal and initiative inspires other workers to greater accomplishments. The major intrigue of the novel revolves either around the formation of such a hero through the awakening of his consciousness of social purpose or the successful efforts of such a hero, already formed, to inspire his fellow-workers with mounting enthusiasm for the job.

The theme of work and production remains important in Soviet literature, and is much more prominent than in Western literature. In some recent fiction, however, there have been important changes in emphasis and focus. Traditionally the Soviet production novel has been loaded with detailed descriptions of industrial processes and working techniques—the operation of railroads, blast furnaces, rolling mills, and electrical circuits. Narrative interest was intended to be derived, in large part, from the intrinsic fascination of the machinery itself, its deployment and maintenance, and from the means of organizing the labor force to meet production quotas. In theory, the production novel was supposed to concentrate on the human element, on the developing psychology and social attitudes of the individual worker, but in practice such novels often degenerated into popular sociotechnological textbooks. Because ideological prescriptions and restrictions made the human element extremely difficult to handle with any degree of persuasiveness, writers tended to avoid human problems by padding their works with industrial detail. Over the years production proved itself to be a limited source of poetry, boring to both writers and readers. Recently many writers have taken to ignoring, purposely, the details of work. Vasili Aksenov's short novel *Oranges from Morocco*, for example, creates an impromptu workers' holiday in which the characters are portrayed at a moment when they are being *distracted* from their labors. They are all good workers, and yet one of them, who works on an oil prospecting rig, wants most of all to leave "this stupendous, enchanting, stinking valley." [11]

Even where work-processes continue to be described, the emphasis is now on the related human drama, the clash of personalities and attitudes, and not on the processes themselves. Georgi Vladimov's *The Big Ore* (translated as *The Ore*),[12] published in 1961, tells vividly and precisely of the difficult techniques of driving a truck up and down the slippery clay slopes of a mining excavation. The descriptions, however, provide a background that makes more convincing the story of a lonely individualist who is so determined to make an outstanding record that, despite his skill and energy, he alienates his fellow truck-drivers. In this, as in other recent stories and novels, the hero is a misfit, an outsider who does not accept the rules, who works well but in an unorthodox manner because he is incapable of adapting himself to the rhythm of the collective. In traditional production novels, such characters either develop proper social attitudes or emerge as clearly-marked villains. Nowadays, however, there is less moral correlation between satisfactory workmanship and other socially desirable qualities. The moral focus of the production theme, in fact, is sometimes in quite another direction. The central character of Voinovich's novel *I Want to Be Honest* (translated as *I'd Be Honest If They'd Let Me*),[13] for example, is a construction supervisor who becomes dispirited in the knowledge that the work going on about him is shoddy, graft-ridden, and ill-conceived, and who, in the long run, can do nothing to correct the situation.

A traditional function of the production novel has been to demonstrate the therapeutic and educational value of work in forming the personality and social outlook of the individual. This didactic element has been particularly prominent in literature about young people. The typical situation has been one in which a youth who has done poorly in school, or who has rebelled against his parents, turns up at some construction site, usually in a remote region. When he first begins working, he is uncooperative, lazy, arrogant, and generally obstreperous. Sooner or later there ensues a crisis, usually involving some construction mishap or particularly challenging production problem, in which, almost against his will, the young hero performs an exploit of courage or quick thinking that discloses his better self. It is revealed that the spirit of the collective has been subtly infecting his rebellious soul. The school of hard knocks, as well as his fellow-workers' example of socialist behavior, has made a man of him, and he is now prepared to re-enter society with a mature and positive outlook on life.

Contemporary Soviet writers still endorse the socialist work-ethic, of course, but they have begun cutting it down to size. This is particularly true of the generation of writers who are now in their twenties and thirties. One Soviet critic has complained that they are "unprepared . . . to take upon themselves the obligation of ideological teachers and educators of their generation." [14] The critic's remarks would seem applicable, for example, to the young Leningrad writer Andrei Bitov, whose short novel *Such a Long Childhood* was published in 1964. The hero, Kirill Kapustin, has been expelled from a mining institute for poor grades. Following an impulse, and without consulting his parents, he joins a group of his former classmates who go to a mining town in the Far North for their required summer of practical experience. When he arrives Kirill writes to his parents and tells them what he has done.

Mama answered him immediately, and he read that she was not angry with him, that they all were very sorry for him, but nevertheless he himself had acted pitilessly in relation to his father, who was so worried about him and was such a sick man, that your things, Kiryusha, I have already collected and will send off tomorrow, and have already sent money by telegram, that at home all are well, that he measure his sleeve length and waist, because she is going to knit him a sweater, because it is very cold in the Polar region, but if he will try, perhaps they will reinstate him, but if nothing works out, don't be upset, because she loves him very much just the same and waits for him, her only son, of her blood, and he should return soon, and she gives him a big, big kiss — mama.

Soon after mama's he received a letter from father, that he is a pup and a greenhorn, and a complete milksop, and let him now try to find out what life is really like, and how he didn't appreciate what they all had done for him, that he was a heartless slob and makes his mother suffer and torment herself, she who is so very sick, that he should expiate his guilt by work and show that he does not bear for nothing the name of the Kapustins, all of whom were very honest working people, but he should nevertheless take care of himself, dress warmly, be careful when he's swimming and watch out for accidents when he's working, that he has sent him money and he's given mother a good fishing rod and tackle to send along with his things, there, they say, they have remarkable fishing, he himself would be glad to come fishing, but he's swamped with work, well, Kirill, behave yourself, I squeeze your hand—papa.[15]

At the mine Kirill becomes an ordinary worker and is gradually estranged from his former classmates: they are going back to school, but he is in the world for good. He accomplishes nothing in particular as a miner. He has an affair—his first—with a local girl, and will presumably marry her. This must wait, however, because he gets drafted. The novel ends as Kirill, with shaven head, marches off with a company of recruits. Experience has matured him somewhat, but the author has this to say about his hero:

It is premature to talk about the beneficial influence of production on the youthful soul, about how this is the way one finds one's place in life. This also is only a stage, and one's place is not found in this way. . . .
Nothing has yet been attained. And there are no guarantees that, having merged himself in the group, he will calm down and distinguish himself from the others — no. And it is also not known whether the moment of parting from childhood—which should have happened many years before and which was moved back and postponed because of circumstances independent of Kirill—is joyful. It remains for those who love him to believe in him, and for others to hope.[16]

Clearly the hero's exposure to socialist production has not worked its traditional magic. Nor should it, Bitov seems to be saying, for the world is not as simple as this.

It should be emphasized that Kirill is not portrayed as a villain or as a failure, a horrible example intended as a warning to young Soviet readers. He is simply an authentic human being, no more and no less. The closing lines of the novel give the author's own appraisal of his hero.

> Kirill Kapustin is leaving with all of them, not really a bad fellow. Not short and not tall. Not fat and not thin. Not handsome and not ugly. Not strong and not weak. Not mature and not a child. With virtues and shortcomings. Big and little. The individual and the multitude. He has already managed to attach himself to something.
>
> He walks away along the road, in the column, with everybody.[17]

The most significant thing about Bitov's character, however, is that by no stretch of the imagination is he a "positive hero." Although the concept of the positive hero remains the most basic element in the structure of socialist realism, and although this mythical paragon of socialist virtues is still the pattern for thousands of Soviet prose writers, in the practice of the best young writers the pattern is disintegrating.

In the words of one Soviet critic who sympathizes with the trend, what is taking place is "not the supplanting of one type of hero by another," but rather "the *enlargement* of the sphere of heroes, expressing the democratization of our life." [18] The stereotype through which the hero emerges from a novel as a well-adjusted, selfless, forward-looking activist, eager to contribute his all to society has been broken up to permit the unrelieved portrayal of a hero who retreats, fails, doubts, or turns from society. There is, in fact, a strong strain of *anti*-heroism among the young writers. Yuri Kazakov, who is probably the most distinguished of them, has created a number of "outsiders" whose most distinguishing traits are misanthropy, self-absorption, or poisonous cynicism. As for the courageous feat or emblematic gesture by means of which the positive hero has traditionally demonstrated his worth, one critic observed in 1962,

> . . . the young writers do not believe in the notion that only he accomplishes a brave exploit who eagerly, easily pronounces lofty words. . . . They are not attracted by this primitive, abstractly derived equation; they want to come to conclusions as a result of their own experience and observations.

This same critic went on to quote Kazakov's own remark that "the life of a man is full of exploits, and this word has been very much loved by our writers. But it is strange that I have never heard it from persons who have accomplished these very exploits." [19]

As a result of attitudes like that of Kazakov, there is a new scepticism, reticence, fear of generalization, and sadness both in the utterances of many recent heroes and in the tones in which they are described. As if to endorse this trend but at the same time to put it to positive use, the young writer Anatoli Kuznetsov has observed that "people are complex and many-sided, and the literature about them should also be thus," but argued that "we must oppose the complicated pessimism of former and contemporary Western literature with our own profound and intelligent optimism." [20] The best writers are obviously having great difficulty in bringing this about, for critics keep complaining of their "one-sided approach to life phenomena" in which the same kinds of "gloomy and musty" episodes recur in story after story, whose authors seem unwilling or unable to "seek a way out of these negative situations which they describe."

In the course of the Stalin period, Russian prose lost much of the rich verbal texture and stylistic variety that had been characteristic of prerevolutionary literature and that of the 1920's. The demands of socialist realism for simplicity and clarity tended to inhibit verbal subtlety and experimentation, and the obligation of ideological indoctrination brought with it a new lexicon of political rhetoric and cant. Under strong semantic controls, the Russian literary language was deprived of much of its liveliness and charm. One of the major developments of recent years has been the move toward restoring the Russian literary language by purging it of a mass of stale, sophistic, sociopolitical epithets, on the one hand, and by infusing it with a fresh stream of natural, colloquial words on the other.

One of the most interesting stylistic features of recent prose has been the revival of the "skaz" manner of narration, which uses colloquial or even vulgar speech that is highly individualized and localized. ("Skaz" was developed by Gogol and Leskov, among others, in the nineteenth century, and was greatly in vogue in the 1920's.) Since the language of "skaz" derives from popular oral usage, it is capable of representing with great fidelity and sensitivity the thoughts and emotions of persons in a particularized social atmosphere. And since it is built upon the speech of an individualized fictitious narrator, it is endowed, when handled well, with a special emotional authenticity and an intimate, eye-witness authority. (*One Day in the Life of Ivan Denisovich* is a brilliant example of the "skaz" manner.) The intensive employment of "skaz" is one of the major weapons which Russian writers are using to combat the artificial and fraudulent locutions of the recent past.

In "skaz,"—usually, though not invariably, a form of first-person narration—the narrator (not the author) is, as a rule, fully and subjectively involved in the story he is recounting. He is a separate character, whose role in the narrative structure is such that there is no way of telling whether or not he reflects the author's own views. The fondness for "skaz" is indicative of a larger trend among contemporary Russian writers to blur the distinction between the author, his narrator, and his characters. Recently Vasili Aksenov observed that "indirect-direct discourse (*kosvenno-pryamaya rech*), a deliberate blending of the author's speech with the speech of the hero, is one of the characteristic peculiarities of contemporary prose." [21] A critic has complained, in this respect, that the "ease and freedom with which the young prose writers conduct first-person narrative is accompanied, as a rule, by a loss of distance between the author and the hero, an uncritical attitude to him." [22] Another observed that "narration now in the person of the hero, now in the person of the author, is surprisingly similar. At times, it even seems that we are hearing the endlessly strung-out monologue of one person." [23]

One can only speculate about this phenomenon. But surely it is related both to the process of purification of language and the new assertiveness of young Russian writers. The cultural authorities have granted writers increased liberty, but not as much as they desire. Through the device of first-person narrator, or "lyrical hero" as he is frequently called, and through the use of reported dialogue and interior monologue, writers can manage to say things without taking direct responsibility for them. The fictitious narrator can utter, in sincere and intimate tones, critical, ironical, or ambiguous opinions which the author would have to disavow explicitly if he were speaking in his own voice. Free of the obligations that must ensue from a narrative posture of omniscience, the author can convey his own irreverence, or even his passionate discontent, through a mask of innocent objectivity. It is this fact that irritates the many politically reactionary Soviet critics who complain that the distinction between the author's voice and that of his characters is being obliterated. Writers should stand up and be counted!

From what has been said above, it might be concluded that young Soviet writers are now engaged in

sly but verbose lyrical outpourings. This is far from
being the case. Actually the language of the young
writers tends to be terse and laconic, full of hints,
unanswered questions, and incompletely-expressed
thoughts. It is a wry, ironical, nervous, sceptical language, one that avoids abstractions and the labels that
suggest ideological formulas. Concerning this trend, a
Soviet critic has remarked:

> . . . we should think thrice before we indict the young
> writers with fear of "lofty words." They do not fear, but
> chastely respect them, they consider that one must have
> a right to "lofty words," and that this right is won by
> deeds. They have a scorn for phrasemakers, for beauti-
> ful-souled babblers, for persons who cover up emptiness
> or indifference with lofty words . . .[24]

The relationship between this new reticence and
the use of a lyrical hero who is close to the author, but
not identifiable as the author, is a most significant one.
A critic who objects to this practice of "fusing the
author with the hero, to whom is given over the right
to perceive and evaluate reality," argues that the
method is "alien to the contemplation of life, to attempts to go outside the frame of the closet experience
of the hero," and indicates a "disbelief in socio-political appraisements, a desire to depart from everything
that constitutes the social-political life of society." [25] A
more sympathetic critic describes this as "a tendency
not to go beyond the boundaries of that which has
been seen with one's own eyes, beyond one's own
tangible experience." [26] Certainly these new esthetic
attitudes come from an unwillingness to indulge in
hackneyed, prefabricated conclusions. To a great extent the writer *is* the hero—shocked, sceptical, trust-
ing only pragmatic experience, wary of officially-
inspired illusions. He contracts his view, draws into
himself, and attentively observes the outside world,
seeing without being seen, as an essential preparation
for the moment when he can come forth with more
valid and more assured truths.

Another indication of the unwillingness, or inability, of young writers to commit themselves to sweeping statements is the decline of the novel in present-day Russia. The huge, exhaustive, majestic exploration and evaluation of life that was inherited from nineteenth-century Russia and cultivated in the Soviet period by such novelists as Sholokhov, Leonov, and Fedin is still being attempted, but the best writers favor the short story or, at most, the short novel (*povest*). The writers still revere Tolstoy and Dostoevsky, but their narrative scope more resembles that of Chekhov. Referring to the current predominance of "small forms," a critic in 1962 argued that "the flowering of the short story has almost always been a sign of the *democratization* of literature, its revival of interest in the life and mores of the people." He added that "the spiritual atmosphere of the 'cult of personality' did not favor the short story—which is so often ironical, sarcastic, morose, 'private' at first glance, seemingly limited," and concluded that, now, "the changing atmosphere of social life nourishes this genre." [27] Many of the best young writers, such as Kazakov, Aksenov, and Voinovich, do not attempt large novels at all, and, with few exceptions, those who write both large novels and shorter works—such as Tendryakov, Daniil Granin, and Soloukhin—are more successful with the latter. But if the short story is a "democratic" form, it does not follow that the novel is intrinsically "undemocratic." It is simply more difficult and dangerous, in uncertain and rapidly changing times, for a democratically-inclined writer to give his views the full exposure that a large novel requires. The novels of Tendryakov, Bondarev, and Solzhenitsyn which I have cited, as well as Konstantin Simonov's recent novels of World War II, do indeed contain bold social criticism, but they enjoy the safety of referring, at least on the surface, to a past era which has been officially condemned.

Meanwhile, in their cultivation of "small forms,"

writers, now that they are freer to recognize that truth is complex and elusive, are experimenting with more subtle and intricate, less direct, and stereotyped narrative means. Many of them, such as Bondarev and Aksenov, write also for the cinema and borrow and rework devices from the films. The stories of Aksenov and Anatoli Gladilin, in fact, sometimes read, to their detriment, like scenarios. The usage of various forms of interior monologue has increased. There is a heavy reliance on dialogue—often slangy, wry, and pungent —to portray circumstances and conflicts that formerly would have been treated through description and analysis. In the hands of a skillful young writer like Voinovich, dialogue reveals the mentality and attitudes of his contemporaries with startling candor, economy, and sensitivity. But also, as a critic observed in 1961, dialogue can be used to excess, to remove authors from difficult situations "when complicated problems arise which they don't know how to solve." [28] The penchant for wise-cracking dialogue has also been critized on other grounds. A heady infatuation with dialogue in the language of the streets has brought about the complaint that vulgar, ephemeral, sub-standard Russian is being perpetuated in literature.

The interest in dialogue, and to a certain extent interior monologue as well, is partly attributable to the influence of such Western writers as Hemingway, Salinger, and Remarque. Writers who use documentary techniques are frequently said to be imitating Dos Passos. The striving for compactness, terseness, and dynamism, and the cultivation of the short sentence, particularly noticeable in the works of younger writers, are all evidence of Western influence. Fifteen years ago it would have been ruinous for a young writer to be found guilty of following Western examples. Today, such influences are freely acknowledged, although there is much unpleasant grumbling from reactionary critics about "the so-called Western style." Some of the experimentation that is tagged as Western in orientation, however, takes its inspiration and many of its models from Russian writers of the nineteen-twenties and early thirties, such as Isaac Babel, Yuri Olesha, and Mikhail Zoshchenko, who were driven out of Soviet literature during the Stalin period.

Associated with all of these stylistic developments, and ultimately the most important feature of contemporary prose, is what the critics call its new "lyricism." As the ideological content of Soviet literature has become less circumscribed, and as its formulas have become less artificial and more flexible, writers have been somewhat freer to seek their own identities, to explore their own psyches, and to work out and express individual sets of values not according to outside prescription, but in accord with their own tastes and private experience. This has introduced a new sincerity, delicacy, and humanity into literature. As one critic phrased it,

> The lyrical form permits one to disclose the finest movements of the soul of the hero, and especially to treat moral problems. . . . Authors turn to the form of the lyrical meditation, to the autobiographical story, and through their own fates and the fates of persons near to them they meditate on the fate of the epoch.[29]

There have been complaints from unsympathetic critics of a creeping "lyrical egocentrism" that threatens to "lock up the narration in the circle of personal impressions of the author." But this is not likely to happen, at least on a wide scale. The opportunities for genuinely full-throated lyricism are limited to those writers who find themselves in a happy state of adjustment to every aspect of Soviet life and of acquiescence to every article of official belief. All others must, either consciously or unwittingly, observe constraints proportionate to the degree of their discontent.

There is lyricism, but it is modulated by reticence. Some things must just not be mentioned. This is why the meditations in the internal monologues of young heroes so frequently stop this side of profundity, or end in queries. This is why it is possible, for example, to insert a sympathetic Jewish character into a novel and to imply (as does Tendryakov in *A Rendezvous with Nefertiti*) that he is the victim of an anti-Semitic act, but not possible to be in any way explicit about it. And this is why many "lyrical heroes" of young authors make wry jokes and seem frequently on the verge of muttering.

In the compactness and brevity of many young writers—Kazakov, Aksenov, Voinovich, and Bondarev are examples—there is a tone sometimes of scepticism, and sometimes of resigned indifference, all as if motivated by the unspoken question: "What are they going to do to me next?" The attitude seems to stem from a sense of being hemmed in, of conscious submission to the necessity of having one's life assigned, and a feeling that one must simply "make do" because circumstances conspire to make it impossible to have one's choices really respected. The dominant mood, however, is not one of stoicism but of a kind of suppressed rage. There seems almost to be a convention, among the young writers, of having the hero get wildly drunk, at least once in the course of a narrative. As a rule it is a mean, destructive drunk, in which he insults and scandalizes everyone about him, stumbles about the streets, and flails blindly at a malevolent world before he passes out. Needless to say, this is not the behavior of a "positive hero." It is, rather, the explosion of a frustrated idealist, whose usual habit of tight-lipped awareness and direct responses has been temporarily conquered by despair. The world is a congenial place for phonies and bastards; one must learn how to spot them and fight them without losing one's head, but occasionally it is just too much.

Moral discovery is in fact the major burden of young Russian writers who write about young people. Voinovich's *Two Comrades* looks at the world through the eyes of Valery Vazhenin, the son of divorced parents, who lives with his mother (an economist) and grandmother, and who occasionally goes across town to visit his father, a pathetic writer of copy for circus acts who is now married to a taunting harridan. Valery loves his mother, although her protectiveness annoys him, and he has a pitying affection for his father; he cannot understand how two such good people can have separated. His narrative covers a period beginning a few months before his induction into the army and ending when he is a full-fledged soldier. The heart of the story, however, is a cluster of episodes in which Valery, wandering about town in a state of mildly rebellious adolescent indecision, begins to grow up. The central episode is one in which he discovers a major moral flaw in his boyhood friend, Tolik.

Late one night Valery and Tolik are accosted on the street by a gang of hoodlums. After a one-sided struggle, they pinion Valery's arms and force Tolik to pound his face to a pulp. A few days later, Valery and Tolik meet at the induction station.

> "Valery," began Tolik, agitated and hunting for words, "you're probably sore at me, but in my place . . ."
> All these days I had been thinking how I would have acted in Tolik's place, whether I could have acted otherwise. And in the end I understood that I could have. And not because I'm so brave, but because I couldn't have done what Tolik did.
> "You understand," he said, "they forced me."
> "Yes, but you really let me have it," I said.
> "But they would have beaten up both you *and* me."
> "O.K.," I said, "We'll talk about it some other time."
> What could I have explained to him?

Months later they meet again, and Valery discovers that Tolik is now a general's orderly and has taken to publishing poetry in praise of his top-sergeant. Tolik again brings up the subject of the beating.

"I've thought a lot about that thing that happened near the Palace . . . Of course I feel bad about it, but that's how it turned out . . ."

"Yes, it's tough," I agreed.

"Yes, a little," said Tolik. "But for you it was better that way."

"Interesting!" I was sincerely surprised. "And just why?"

"They would have hit you harder," he said, looking me straight in the eye.

This was philosophy already. Later I met up with it in other circumstances, heard approximately the same words from other persons who hastened to do what anybody else would have done in their place.

The episode of the beating is thus raised to a symbolic level. It has a universal moral meaning, of course, but it has a special significance in an authoritarian society which is burdened with a history of debilitating rationalizations, and in which the individual has all too frequently signed over his ethical responsibilities to the collective.

But the story of Voinovich is not as gloomy as the quoted passages might indicate. It also has a brisk, rollicking, good-natured self-mocking quality that comes from the bright and attractive personality of its narrator (who is, incidentally, reading *The Catcher in the Rye*). His grandmother has read the New Testament to him as a boy. Somehow he is reminded of this as he takes his first airplane ride:

I had a condescending attitude toward grandmother's religious fancies, especially after the seventh grade, when our chemistry teacher Leonila Maksimovna . . . by means of certain chemical experiments demonstrated the indubitable absence of God. I had long since ceased to believe in God, but the fact that everything relating to God was written there in capital letters still pleased me. On occasion I wanted to write about myself in similar style. For example, when they seated me in the airplane: "And they took Him by His Hand, placed Him in the cockpit. And His Shoulders and His Stomach and all His Body they fastened with straps."

The story of Voinovich illustrates not only the fact that the present generation of young Soviet writers has turned with fresh intensity to problems of conscience, trust, honor, decency, justice, and loyalty, but also that it displays an increased interest in human beings, not as they should be, but as they are. Sexual infidelity and the eternal triangle, long considered frivolous and even harmful topics for Soviet literature, are accepted as intrinsically interesting and self-justifying. Psychological problems can now be depicted in detail, provided they are not apprehended in total divorcement from the social context. The conflict between parents and children—a favorite theme of the young writers —can now be depicted not only as a product of social change (which indeed it is), but also as something inherent in the human psyche. There is a more tolerant interest in human error and inadequacy, and a greater freedom to portray maladjustment, neurosis, and personal conflicts without making moral judgments or coming up with pat solutions. The individual is important not only because he has a function in society, but also because he has a soul. A critic has observed that in Soviet literature until recently,

> a man's occupation was higher and more significant than the man himself . . . A man's "line of work" served as his intellectual characteristic. The possibility of the arising of the question—*is the work higher than the man or the man higher than his work*—is a peculiarity of recent years.[30]

A striking indication of the new humaneness of Soviet literature is the fact that, at least among the best writers, the Communist Party has virtually disappeared from fiction. Until the middle-fifties, party cadres were omnipresent in works with a contemporary setting—solving problems, giving sage advice, inspiring by example, and often performing the role of a kind of collective *deus ex machina*. In the interests of "realism," of course, it was necessary to attempt to characterize party members as human beings, warts and all. But since they had a special moral function in the narrative, the temptation to sentimentalize them, or to make them unnaturally gallant, was usually far too powerful to overcome. In actuality, the Party still dominates public life, and the proportion of characters in present-day literature who happen to be Communists may well be nearly as large as it ever was. The difference is that they are not named as such. There are probably two reasons for this phenomenon. First, the liberalization of literary controls has made it easier for writers to portray examples of unpunished evil behavior on the part of characters in positions of responsibility, but to identify them specifically as Party members, which they undoubtedly are, would be to go beyond the permissible limits of candor. Second, and more important, the new comparative freedom to treat humans as humans and not as social symbols, and the removal of the pressure on literature to trumpet the glory of the Communist Party, have combined to permit the lifting of the party label from fictional characters.

Where the party has moved out of literature, the folk have moved in. The broader examination of national life, and the study of the peculiarities of its individual regions and byways that is being carried on largely through the medium of documental prose, has its fictional counterpart in the rediscovery of the backwaters. Local color and folk characters have always been present in Soviet fiction. Now, however, writers of fiction are exploring the peasant village and emphasizing, not so much the changes that have been wrought by socialism, but rather the continuing harshness of peasant life. Kazakov, Abramov, and Alexander Yashin, among others, have shown, in a manner that approaches naturalism, the deprivation and discontent in the countryside, but also the stubborn endurance of peasant psychology and culture that antedates the revolution. Perhaps the finest story in recent years is Solzhenitsyn's *Matryona's Home*, whose heroine is a humble and superstitious peasant widow,—a hard-working and totally selfless soul, exploited by her neighbors. Like many other peasant characters in current Soviet fiction, Matryona is a throwback to the peasants of Turgenev, Tolstoy, and Chekhov. The increased fidelity and humanity of Russian literature has enabled writers to show that, at least in the countryside, the Russian character has been little touched by the revolution.

Despite the accomplishments of the past fifteen years, Soviet prose still has not regained the distinction it enjoyed in the 1920's. Among the hundreds of young writers who are now being published, there are a dozen or so who, if given the opportunity, could grow to major stature, but a new Isaac Babel, Yuri Olesha, or Evgeny Zamyatin does not seem to be on the horizon at present. Solzhenitsyn is no longer a "young writer," but it is quite possible that if he should be allowed to publish several works that he is reported already to have written it will be discovered that he is indeed a great writer. The talents of Andrei Sinyavsky and Yuli Daniel have been sealed off in a concentration camp. Many others, no doubt, are still writing "for the drawer," and it is possible that censorship prohibits the publication of still others.

The real leaders of Soviet literature in recent times have been the poets. An explanation of this phenomenon is outside the scope of the present effort, and would be speculative at best. But the very nature of present literary conditions is such that poetry, in which vagueness, subtlety, and multiplicity of meanings are permitted, can manage to convey the complicated thoughts and feelings of contemporary Russians more effectively than prose, which can be forced to be more explicit and is more easily "censorable." The greater tangibility of prose, and the mode of "realism" to which it is presently restricted, make it more vulnerable to the kinds of controls which the state still applies to it.

This is why the Soviet novel is presently inadequate as a full statement and evaluation of experience. Too many of the questions that have always made writing interesting—for example the nature of evil—are still governed by prescribed answers. (One looks in vain, for example, for a Soviet Camus: even Camus the original is unavailable to Soviet writers.) There are too many frozen propositions about history and social relationships that must still remain unchallenged. As a consequence, most Soviet long prose works are repetitious and boring, and tend to fence with problems rather than come to grips with them. Soviet writers are constantly urged to study the narrative techniques of Tolstoy, but they are prohibited from emulating his searching, sceptical intelligence.

The very terseness of many of the best young writers, and their preference for short forms, is not only a result of their urge to avoid the ponderous, pompous falsity of the recent past but also of their realization that under present circumstances the price of survival is to write suggestively rather than explicitly, and impressionistically rather than exhaustively.

In his brilliant essay "On Socialist Realism," [31] Sinyavsky suggests that the rehabilitation of Soviet literature be based not on a return to critical realism, but rather on a development of the grotesque, the absurd, and the fantastic. It would appear, however, that the long-established tastes and ideological fears of the cultural authorities will prevent this, that in the foreseeable future Soviet literature will remain conservative in form and style, and that the best practical hope lies in an increase in the tendency toward critical realism. In terms of Western literary development, this may well be an anachronism. But a turning-back of the cultural clock by half a century is scarcely too high a price to pay for a restoration of the ability to tell the unvarnished truth.

The French Novel
Quests and Questions

WALLACE FOWLIE

During the years immediately following the Liberation, 1945–50, existentialism dominated French intellectual and artistic life. It annexed to its philosophical
works the domains of the novel and the theatre. It
even appropriated a political role and played it alternately in agreement with or in opposition to Marxism.
At the same time, the term designated far more than a
fictional or dramatic form, far more than a program of
moral philosophy. Cafés were known as existentialist,
and ways of dressing, in a casual if not rudimentary
fashion, and ways of wearing one's hair, were called
existentialist. Today, ten to fifteen years later, it is
easier to make out the full significance of existentialist
doctrine, as it appeared especially in novels, plays, and
literary criticism, between 1945 and 1950. Its importance is verifiable in the way it has continued to influence the art of fiction since 1950.

For Jean-Paul Sartre, the immediate datum is existence, when it is felt through the experience of anguish.
His philosophy affirms the sovereignty of man's conscience, and the presence of the world. He claims that
man's existence excludes the existence of God, that
man is his own future, that he is what he makes of
himself. Such concepts have been studied and often
adhered to by the novelists. The experience of the
absurd, so often referred to by Sartre and Camus,
constitutes a critical approach to the world, a stage in
life that has to be acknowledged and lived through.

The older values of good and evil are rejected by Sartre as being erroneously absolute. The new Sartrian value is a man's project and not the good or evil he does.

This philosophy has been so compelling that it has appeared in various ways in the French novel, and especially of course in the writings of Sartre himself, in *La Nausée* (*Nausea*), the novel of 1938, in *Le Mur* (*The Wall*), the collection of stories of 1939, and in the three volumes of the unfinished novel, *Les Chemins de la liberté* (1945–51; *The Roads to Freedom*). Albert Camus' awareness of the absurdity of life, led him to the idea that man is free to live as he wishes. In *L'Etranger* (*The Stranger*) of 1942 and *La Peste* (*The Plague*) of 1947, he looks upon human nature as a value that gives to action its meaning and its limitations. The impersonal simple style of Camus, with its clipped almost monotonous notations, seems today inseparable from the atmosphere of the absurd as it is created and recreated in later novels and plays.

The traditional use of the novel as diversion and entertainment, as an indulgence in sentimentality for the reader, has given way to a new means of communication between intellectuals of one country, such as France, and intellectuals of several other countries. By 1950, the novel had been quite firmly established as an expression of deep-seated worries, of responsibilities, of moral problems, and religious preoccupations that are central to an entire generation. It has become international: the French novels are translated almost immediately into several languages and are read by the same kind of public in several countries who welcome the books as novels but also as instruments of communication.

The new form of fiction that has been developing in France, which is perhaps not as new as some spokesmen have claimed, reflects everything, even if it does not comment on everything: the inventions of the day, the political impasses of the day; the current

views on man's fate, the fashions of dress and manners
and philosophies, the research carried out in psychology, sociology, anthropology, ethnology. Very often
the new writer has a second métier which may be
reflected in the style and content of his novels. Novels,
plays, and films are more closely related than ever
before, and the novel often seems to be written with a
theatrical and film adaptation in mind. The novel
derives from everything: from ideas and manners,
from politics and science, and it gives back this varied
nourishment in forms that are narration and commen-
tary and interpretation, but explicitly, never cumber-
somely so.

The entire history of the French novel might be
written in terms of the ever increasing degree of self-
revelation the novelist gives of his characters and of
himself. Up until today, the major French novels have
been studies about the inner life of man, analyses of
motivations and sentimental reactions. This form is as
true of *La Princesse de Clèves* in the seventeenth
century, as it is of *Manon Lescaut* in the eighteenth,
of Proust and Mauriac and Genet in the twentieth.
Aspects of society are described in all of these novels.
With Proust, and to some degree with the so-called
"new" novelists, society is questioned more than it is
described. And the questions imply judgments. In
Proust, the immodesty of the self-revelation is far
greater than that in Mme. de La Fayette, in Laclos, in
Balzac, and in Zola. Gide spoke of "sincerity" rather
than of "immodesty" when he analyzed the modern
writer's effort to tell everything about himself. Rousseau's claim, in the opening sentence of *Les Confessions*, that no one will ever speak as openly or as
truthfully about himself as he does, is invalidated by
such novelists as Lawrence, Wolfe, Miller outside of
France, and by almost all of the major French writers
of the past fifty years, since *Du Côté de chez Swann*
appeared in 1913.

Intimacy, and the most secret kind of intimate revelations, have developed within the novel, as the genre itself has developed. This practice has turned the reader into a kind of *voyeur* or vampire. It often creates within the reader a worry that the pleasure he derives from reading novels is sinful or immoral. From Rousseau on, who announced it blatantly, through Zola, Gide, Mauriac and even today with Nathalie Sarraute, the temptation to write about the most intimate secrets of man, has become a veritable obsession. The art of the novel is today totally indiscreet in that it attempts to communicate to the reader emotions and instincts and acts that in the past have been looked upon as incommunicable.

In such a novel as *La Nausée,* a key text for the development of the French novel since 1950, the study of a character's conscience is an extraordinary document, and was, in 1938, when it first appeared, quite new. The analysis of Roquentin's conscience is more basic, more distressingly personal than any analysis of his sensations or his feelings would be. Sartre gives in this novel a vivid concrete description of the uselessness of a man's memories, of the sense of hollowness, emptiness, indecisiveness, solitude, that lie at the very heart of a man's nature. The subject matter of *La Nausée* marks a turning point in the history of the novel. It represents an heroic effort to define a man's destiny.

More lucidly than Sartre, Albert Camus illustrates in his writing the central paradox of the novel, and of all art, for that matter. Camus believed that art performs simultaneously two functions: that of exalting and that of negating. The novelist, and especially the existentialist novelist, refuses the world as it is, and calls upon another kind of world to replace it. This dual action is of course in the word *revolt,* used so often by both Sartre and Camus. The artist attempts to remake a world by depending upon the reality of a world he wants to eradicate. The novel thus brings us back to the origins of revolt, insofar as it tries to give form to a value that is constantly changing because it is involved in the passing of time. The novelist (the artist) attempts to steal from time that which time eventually will demolish. The paradox is stated throughout the writings of Camus, especially in his last two books: the novel *La Chute* (*The Fall*) of 1956, and the collection of stories, *L'Exil et le Royaume* (*Exile and the Kingdom*) of 1957. He shows us man refusing to accept the world as it is, and at the same time refusing to escape from the world. This paradox actually describes the two extreme forms of the novel, applicable throughout the entire history of the novel: the depiction of the real world, or what is called realism, and the depiction of man's flight into an imaginary or a fantasy world.

Both Sartre and Camus acknowledged the debt they owed the hard realistic American novels of the thirties, whose characters were described solely in terms of their behavior and their exterior actions and reactions. In their writing, however, Sartre and Camus went beyond the limitations of American realism in their effort, precisely, to follow the conscience of their characters and to describe the significance of the world which a man's conscience could give to him.

More than Sartre, Camus realized that art imposes on the writer the need to choose and discard. His theories are close to the classical concept of art where there has to be a subject matter taken from the world and which is transfigured by the form the artist imposes on it. Camus' esthetics parallels his view of society and his philosophy of man where antithesis is the guiding principle. In his art as a novelist and as a man deeply committed to the problems of his day, Camus illustrated the antithesis of refusal and consent, of individualism and universality, of artifice and nature, of the passions in man aroused by night, and the hope of clear thinking stimulated by the noonday sun. The novelist is the artist concerned centrally with the tension that is generated between the individual man and history. In order to reach this extreme equilibrium or balance, the artist must refuse nothing from life but he must not take everything from it.

The character of *La Chute*, Jean-Baptiste Clamence, is the type of man opposite to Camus' early hero Meursault in *L'Etranger*. He is keenly aware of all the modern forms of servitude, willing to "play the game," precisely that game of society Meursault would not play, unable to find the moral absolutes he needed. Amsterdam, with its dark stone canals is the same kind of inferno for Clamence that the real prison was for Meursault at the end of *L'Etranger*. Clamence asks what meaning his life must have if he is not to lie to himself. The conclusion of the book seems to state that a man cannot judge evil in the name of the good which he himself does not represent. All he can hope to do is to discern evil, and in himself first, in order to denounce it.

If there is a *summa* in the writings of Albert Camus, it is *La Chute*, the most violent of his books, written with exceptional mastery over his craft and involving an expression of ambiguity over man's life on this earth, an ambiguity which is, after all, one of the characteristics of the new novel in France. In this period covering the last fifteen or twenty years, such mastery over form and theme as is found in *La Chute* has not been achieved except in the cases of Beckett and Genet.

How can this ambiguity be defined? Clamence is a man who multiplies his confessions throughout the book, for this is a story told by one voice in an ill-famed bar in Amsterdam. It is a single voice with a multiplicity of tones: scornful, satiric, proud, complaining, anguished. The book is a story, but it is also an essay, an allegory, a philosophical tale. So, in the first place, the genre of *La Chute* is ambiguous, and this characteristic will be true of *L'Innommable* (*The*

Unnamable) of Beckett, of *Miracle de la Rose* of Genet, of *L'Ecluse* of Jean-Pierre Faye.

A single word, the title, is the major clue: *la chute*. It is the confession of a man fallen from grace, expelled from Eden, that is, from Paris where he had been a successful lawyer, admired, and loved. Amsterdam is his purgatory, if not his hell, where he calls himself a penitent: *un juge-pénitent*. He is there because of a mysterious laughter he had heard in Paris, an obscure occurrence that initiated in him a painful inner debate. He lives now, outside of Eden, with the knowledge he is guilty. His conscience has been awakened and therefore he has lost his peace of mind. This *inquiétude*, deliberately or unconsciously instigated, is a major theme in the modern novel, and has been especially analyzed by Gide, Sartre, and Camus.

The French call it *la mauvaise conscience*, which is the theme of Clamence's confession and which he slowly unmasks. Camus prolonged the work of Gide and of the more strictly Christian novelist Bernanos, by his determination to uncover the truth about man's moral dilemmas and moral dramas. He did not despair over man any more than Gide or Bernanos did, and he denounced as vigorously as they did, the false hopes of modern man. *La Chute* takes its place beside *Les Faux-Monnayeurs* of Gide (1925) and *Sous le soleil de Satan* of Bernanos (1926) as a study of the duplicity inherent in man's character whereby evil borrows the ways and the arguments of truth and God. The pessimism of Camus' writing—very much in evidence in *La Chute*—is always in terms of man's frauds and impostures.

When *La Chute* appeared in 1956, Camus was a famous writer, widely recognized and admired throughout Europe and America. Five years earlier, in 1951, Samuel Beckett published his novel *Molloy* which may in time occupy a more important place in the evolution of the French novel. By 1951, many of the hopes that had flourished at the time of the Liberation, had vanished. Sartre had not continued his novel, of which the third volume, *La Mort dans l'âme* (*Death in the Soul*, translated as *Iron in the Soul*), had been printed in 1946. He was giving his attention almost exclusively to political problems: to denunciations of nuclear warfare and to the Algerian crisis. Many French intellectuals were disillusioned, especially those close to existentialism and left-wing ideology. This disillusionment is graphically described by Mme Simone de Beauvoir in her novel of 1954, *Les Mandarins*.

Beckett was quite unknown in 1951. *Molloy* appeared almost simultaneously with the first books of the new novelists Nathalie Sarraute and Robbe-Grillet. Characteristics of the new novel had already been noticed in the writings of Joyce, Kafka, and Faulkner, and also in such French works as *La Nausée* and *L'Etranger*. All of these writers wanted to purify the novel of elements that did not belong to the genre. Beckett's role in this enterprise is central. It is quite possibly the major role. His effort of purification, usually called a demolishing of the novel, was the continuation of the great prewar novelists, such as Joyce and Faulkner.

After *Molloy* had been refused by six Paris publishers, it was accepted by Jérôme Lindon, of the Éditions de Minuit, who was to welcome other new novelists and become a recognized publisher of the works of Robbe-Grillet, Butor, Sarraute, Pinget, Duras. He published *En attendant Godot* (*Waiting for Godot*) in 1952, and the play, since its first performances in 1953, has brought world fame to Beckett.

Sartre, in denouncing Mauriac as the type of omniscient novelist, set a new mode with *La Nausée*, in which the novelist does not pretend to explain anything. This is the mode of writing that *Molloy* continues. It is sufficient for the character of a novel to describe what he sees and feels. If he sees and feels very little, even nothing, that will be enough too for the novel to relate. When the first critics began paying attention to *Molloy*, they tended to use such a term as "nihilistic" in describing the work. The nihilism of *La Nausée* and *L'Etranger* had already been pointed out, but for Sartre and Camus, this attitude was used as a preliminary stage in their philosophy, as a way of ultimately finding a meaning for existence.

A search for meaning is not apparent in Beckett. He discards, refuses, denounces, in a peaceful manner. As he demolishes the world existing around man, he builds up in his art of a novelist, a structure of words. His is the novel of language, the kind of novel that Flaubert once said he wished he could write: the novel about nothing (*le livre sur rien*).

Molloy and all the novels of Beckett are about obsessions that actually take the place of the characters and events we follow in the traditional kind of novel. Therefore, what can be called the story in *Molloy* is confusing and incomplete. By definition, an obsession is nothing, because it is imaginary. In writing about obsessions, Beckett will inevitably end by writing more about language than about events and characters. It is not as important to see physical traits of the characters Molloy and Moran (who may well be the same man) as to continue hearing them speak, and following their search, whatever this search is and even if it is totally vain. In the traditional novel, the hunter is easily distinguished from the hunted, but in Beckett they resemble one another. The master and slave are easily confused. The action of the story does continue in its own way, but it tends to move back to the beginning. An event becomes a mirror in which an earlier event is visible.

The story itself of a Beckett novel is in a constant state of precariousness. A discourse starts up strongly, then weakens and stops, only to start up again with similar phrases. But since there is no need to convince the reader of a chronological sequence, or of the relative importance of events, all precision of structure tends to vanish. The opening of a passage is usually strong and forthright, as in the first sentence of the book. *Je suis dans la chambre de ma mère*. But as the sentences continue, it is difficult to see a sequence in them, a relationship between them. It is the voice that counts in the long monologue, the sound of the voice. There is something of a story, but it seems to be going on outside of the monologue. The phrases of the text are not related to the experience that is being lived, and we can only half suspect what this experience is. The real experience is being denied by the immediate experience of the words on the page which we are forced to read. The language of the words removes us from the language of the experience. This is perhaps the supreme form of literary language that exists for and by itself.

There is so little form in the traditional sense of form, that the paucity of form becomes all important, and one's attention is riveted to it. The two characters, for example, Molloy and Moran, call up in the reader's mind such a question as: what is their relationship? Is Moran merely the conscience of Molloy? Are they the same man in search of himself? This very difficulty of seizing the relationship is an intriguing exercise for the reader. Beckett makes the discovery that it is impossible to narrate what one sees and feels. In the course of the narration, the thing observed becomes something else. Writing becomes therefore an invention. The writer loses interest in the story, and begins writing something else. In other words, the story inevitably breaks down. *Molloy* is precisely about the dispersal of a story. It is also about the dispersal of a life, because the story was to be about the life of Molloy.

Beckett's obsession with the verb *finir* is one of the clues to his kind of novel, as well as to his plays. There is no such thing as an ending for the writer. He has to

go on. The process of disintegration is endless. With
the publication of each book of Beckett, critics have
tended to say: this is the last stage, it is impossible to
go farther in this experience of disintegration. But the
critics have been in error. What they define as an
ending is merely the way leading toward another ending. Beckett is not the first to point out that every
moment in life is an ending. And every moment in life
is a beginning. The title of Beckett's play *Fin de
Partie* (*Endgame*) is significant in this regard. Beckett
would agree with the philosophers and other observers
of the human condition, that man is fated to come to
an end. And yet, as long as he is, he cannot come to an
end. To rephrase all this argument in Beckett's own
terms, we might say that man is that being who cannot imagine his ending.

In this theme telling us there is no way for a man to
come to an end, there is no precise sense of desolation
or of tragedy. On the contrary, the reader becomes
aware of a form of peacefulness presiding over the
fragments of a story. If Molloy tried to be someone, if
he tried to tell a real story, perhaps there might
be tragedy, or a conflict that would culminate in
tragedy.

Dire, c'est inventer. "To speak is to invent." In its
aphoristic bareness, this sentence from *Molloy* is a
kind of motto for Beckett's art, and to some degree,
for the art of the new novel. We often have the
illusion of inventing, Beckett goes on to say, but isn't
it merely a series of fragments of a rehearsed lesson?
This is a disconcerting confession for a writer to make,
and critics are still asking Beckett and other novelists
close to Beckett's literary theories, why they write. If
one story is as good to tell as any other, then why tell
any story at all?

André Gide, in *Les Faux-Monnayeurs* (*The Coun-
terfeiters*), deliberately wrote a novel whose narration
would resemble life in the sense of representing a large
number of episodes and themes that begin but do not

necessarily continue for long or reach any kind of conclusion. Characters appear, disappear, and reappear as they do in life, without always having a relationship with other characters. Beckett's art is far more bare than Gide's, but we find ourselves, when we read these books, in the same labyrinthine world where ways do not lead to a goal, where they begin and then merge into other beginning ways.

The intricacy of situations, and the good tone of humor arising from unexpected encounters are quite similar in *Les Faux-Monnayeurs* and Beckett's first novel *Murphy* which he wrote first in English and then translated into French in 1947. The characters of Gide search for a meaning to their actions and motivations but Beckett's seem to have moved beyond the search and are guided more and more by the simple discovery of humor in the contradictions of existence and in the unpredictable encounters they make. In a more desultory fashion than the Gidian characters represent, Beckett's characters allow projects to form and then almost immediately embark upon the opposite kind of project. What was once treated with great precision of outline in Balzac and Flaubert, becomes nebulous, vague, obscure in Beckett: sentiments, passions, places, even physical traits of the characters. The imprecision of the figures and the ever-changing atmosphere where the figures are, give us, as we read Beckett, the impression of inhabiting a world close to insanity. Or is it the world seen with the clear vision of sanity? At any rate, it is a world devoid of affirmations.

Samuel Beckett's very special power as a novelist is to lead us into such a world where man's condition appears absurd and insignificant. Within that world where he carefully installs us, Beckett keeps telling us he hopes to clarify matters. This hope, however, is never realized, probably because such a realization belongs to another domain than that of the novelist.

At the end of his life, James Joyce befriended Beckett, and undoubtedly his influence was great on his friend and exile—like himself—from Ireland. However, in choosing French as his language, Beckett moved in an opposite direction from Joyce who had enriched the English language with many other languages in order to create a varied and fertile verbal substance. To begin with, French is not as rich as English, and Beckett's French is even more reduced to a basic kind of language that appears logical and clear. Whereas Beckett is a fervent admirer of Joyce and Proust, his style of writing, in its arch-simplicity, in its lack of poetry, in its monotony and repetitiousness, is the opposite of theirs. Beckett dwells on the infirmities of his characters, on their physical degradation. This would seem to be his accusation against life. If there is an accusation in Proust and Joyce, it is of a moral and psychological and spiritual order. Beckett's sentences come from this movement of physical disintegration that he studies in book after book. He creates first in his characters an obsession with the world about them, and then he seems to undertake very slowly and imperceptibly the destruction of that world.

The novels of Jean Genet were not made accessible to the general public until 1951, when the Gallimard edition of his works began appearing. The same year, therefore, saw the publication of Beckett's *Molloy*, with its emphasis on man's defeat and failure, on man as an infirm vagabond recalling his life as a long confused emotion in a world that has no meaning, and the publication of Genet's *Miracle de la Rose*, where a criminal is given the status of an aristocrat, of a sovereign lord. In the same year, these two novelists gave the two pictures of a dehumanized hero and a sanctified hero.

The concept of sovereignty has always obsessed the imagination of Genet. Sartre believes that Genet chose evil because that was precisely the realm in which he could hope to reach a status of sovereignty. In *Miracle de la Rose*, in those passages where the character Harcamone is meditating in his cell, the ideal of sovereignty is ascribed to the assassin who is about to be executed. The state of evil is the reverse of the state of holiness. Genet plays on the two worlds because he finds them similar in the sense that the extremes of both are forbidden to an ordinary man, and that both are characterized by violence and danger.

The theory of alienation is prevalent in contemporary literature, and it has never been orchestrated so richly, with such tragic and sensual poignancy, as in Genet's books. The existences evoked in his novels and plays, which are obviously his own existence, cannot find their realization. These characters fully understand how estranged, how alienated they are, and they are both obsessed and fascinated by this state.

Genet began writing in prison with the avowed purpose of composing a new moral order which would be his. His intention was to discover and construct a moral order that would explain and justify his mode of life. All of his early commentators spoke, with considerable wonderment, of two matters in particular: the unusual boldness of Genet's themes, which would seem at that time, in the middle forties, to exclude the books forever from accessible editions, and the ease with which this writer, from the very start, from his first novel, wrote in a style and with a profundity of thought which placed him in the category of "great writers." To reach, with so little preparation, the highest rank in literary art, was almost as shocking to the first readers of Genet, as his obvious determination to glorify evil as it appears in those forms that are the most rigorously castigated by society.

Genet celebrates those particular manifestations of evil which he knew personally. The central drama is always the struggle between the man in authority and the young man to whom he is attracted. The psychological variations of this struggle are many. Each of the novels is a different world in which the same drama unfolds. *Querelle de Brest* is the ship: naval officers and sailors. *Pompes Funèbres* (*Funeral Rites*) is the Occupation: Nazi officers and young Frenchmen of the capital. *Notre-Dame-des-Fleurs* is Montmartre, with its world of male prostitutes and pimps. *Miracle de la Rose* is the prison, with the notorious criminals and their slaves.

The hallucinatory beauty with which Jean Genet has expressed his system of morality and his philosophy of evil increases the difficulty of defining his tradition and assessing his worth. He is the arch-romantic, far more the artist than the philosopher. His nature is essentially religious. His is also a nature of extreme passivity. In this sense, he is more comparable to Baudelaire than to Rimbaud or Lautréamont. He is the opposite of the revolutionist and the reformer. He is the man living just outside of the normally-constituted society. He has no desire to play a part in society, especially no desire to mount in society, to triumph over it. He is therefore the opposite of Balzac's Rastignac and Stendhal's Julien Sorel.

Genet had the good fortune to attract the attention of Jean-Paul Sartre who, in a six-hundred-page book, *Saint Genet, comédien et martyr*, elaborately analyzes why he believes that Jean Genet incarnates existentialist freedom. After giving himself over to what the world calls crime and evil, Genet turned to writing, and in rapid succession produced novels that are apologies for evil. By becoming a writer, he exercised his freedom, according to Sartre, chose his own life and defined himself.

This experience of Genet is the basis of Sartre's long investigation into the problem of evil. The philosopher does not conceal the shocking elements in the writings of Genet. He uses them in a purely philosophical way in order to describe the human anguish of this man. Sartre never forgets that the subject of his study is a man ostracized by society. He finds in Genet's revindication of evil the only form of dignity vouchsafed to him.

The term "anti-novel" (*anti-roman*) was invented by Sartre in a preface he wrote for Nathalie Sarraute's novel *Portrait d'un inconnu* (*Portrait of a Man Unknown*), first published in 1949, and reprinted by Gallimard in 1957. Mme Sarraute, with Alain Robbe-Grillet and Michel Butor, are the chief theorists and practitioners of the *nouveau roman*. The movement derives from existentialist theories expressed during the forties, and possibly from the poems of Francis Ponge who has devoted his art to the description of objects, and who has been praised by both Sartre and Camus. The books of the three novelists are not similar, and often their theories about the art of the novel are so contradictory that it is difficult to think of them as representing a coherent school of writing.

They look upon the new novelists as continuing the work of Joyce and Proust, but in a totally different way. Between Balzac and Proust, the novelist presented in his work types of characters clearly drawn and clearly explained by the psychological life of the characters. Nathalie Sarraute claims that this kind of writing is over, that new domains and new techniques must be discovered by the new novelists. Her ambition is to explore that minute world, that very obscure world in a human being where thought and impulses first form, and which are constantly disappearing and rebeginning. The novelist must look intently (this group of writers have been called *l'école du regard*) at the most minute things: an imperceptible tenseness in a face, the twitching of a muscle, an insignificant object that somehow gives assurance, the minor attacks or innuendos that people give one another.

The biological term *tropismes*, used by Mme Sarraute as the title of her first book (published in 1938, reprinted in 1957, Editions de Minuit), designates the minute changes in a human being taking place each second, the residue of words spoken, the nuances of sentiments like the shadings of light that come and go, the network of banalities in which a figure is caught, the particles of thought and conviction and sentiment that adhere to us without our realizing it. The novelist intervenes in all this, to ask questions, to track down motivations, to follow after the dispersal of words and feelings. It is a form of inquest, of interrogation he carries on, as he unmasks the characters, and he is often caught as they are by the slow-moving accretion of time and habit.

Le Planétarium, of 1959, illustrates Mme Sarraute's consummate skill in organizing a novel around hundreds of details minutely placed together. It is an admirable text by which to judge what is new in the technique of the novel, and what has been carried over from the traditional form of fiction. The stream of consciousness (le monologue intérieur) is used throughout Le Planétarium, an art-form lavishly orchestrated by Virginia Woolf and in a much more diffuse way than in Mme Sarraute's novel, whose style is more rational, more clipped, more precise. In Faulkner and Proust, as well as in Virginia Woolf, the normal flow of time is often interrupted and the past is brought into the present. Episodes that had taken place in the past are joined with episodes taking place in the present, in order to offer a total picture of life. In contrast with that art, Nathalie Sarraute's novel is rigorously chronological. The action begins one evening and ends a few months later, after a series of successive episodes that are described by means of fragments of a stream of consciousness.

Le Planétarium shows Mme Sarraute to be a novelist untouched by those multiple poetic elements that constitute a large part of the twentieth-century novel: Proust, in particular, but also Barrès, Gide, Alain-Fournier, Saint-Exupéry, Colette, and countless others. Proust was the great master of that technique whereby the sudden appearance of a church steeple in a country landscape forced the hero into a descent into himself, into a vision of the world where space and time, in their usual connotations, are abolished. Such passages, rightfully called poetic, are absent from the books of Mme Sarraute. As a novelist, she is intent upon perceiving the relationships between human beings, and the relationships between a human being and the world he inhabits. No one of her characters inhabits exactly the same world, and yet it is the same world common to the characters. And no one character is the same for anyone else. Each character of *Le Planétarium* is uneasy because of the anxiety he feels in the presence of others, even members of his family, and because of the need he has for others. This anxiety, analyzed in a masterful way, is mysterious, and yet the work itself is never obscure. The writing is direct, the language is simple, without trace of preciosity.

Mme Sarraute has written and spoken quite extensively about her understanding of the novel, and many of her arguments and theories help to clarify the ambitions of the novelists who have been writing during the past fifteen years. She has pointed out that there are basically two kinds of reality for the writer. First, the reality in which he lives, visible to everyone, that is known or easily knowable, a reality that has been expressed over and over again, and which is the province of the journalist or the reporter or the documentary expert. But this is not the reality that interests or attracts the novelist. That second reality or domain is what is not yet known, not yet visible, and therefore it is what cannot be easily expressed. The art of the novelist does not restore what is visible, it makes something visible. What is this reality? It is infinitely difficult to define because it is so diffused, so vague, so amorphous, so deprived of ordinary existence. It is a conglomeration of possibilities which are covered over precisely by that other kind of reality which is visible, known, articulated.

The novels of Alain Robbe-Grillet are very different from those of Nathalie Sarraute, but the two writers have similar attitudes toward traditional literature. They both know that great novels of the past have been based upon visible reality and have treated political, social, and moral issues related to that reality. Sartre continued that tradition in what he calls *littérature engagée*. Robbe-Grillet and Sarraute, as well as Butor, Simon, and Pinget, testify to the need to transform the novel and develop technical aspects instigated by the three great revolutionists in the first quarter of the twentieth century: Proust, Joyce, and Kafka. The literary school of the *nouveau roman* claims that the writer moves naturally from the visible to the invisible. These experimental writers are thereby led to further discoveries of still more unknown realities in man.

After his first two works, *Les Gommes* of 1953 and *Le Voyeur* of 1955, Robbe-Grillet published an article (*Une voix pour le roman futur, La Nouvelle Revue Française*, July 1956) in which he says that the world for him is neither meaningful (*signifiant*) nor absurd. It simply *is*. His third book, *La Jalousie* of 1957, marks a culminating point in his search for his type of novel, in which the world resembles a spectacle from which he as narrator is almost totally eliminated. In this case, the "world" is a banana plantation in the tropics, a married woman, and a friend of the husband and wife who is carrying on an illicit relationship with the woman. All of that is made visible, but the man who is looking at it, and who is the husband and narrator, is not visible. We see only what he sees and we soon realize that his glance (his *regard*) deforms everything. The book's title plays on the two meanings of "jealousy" and "Venetian blind." The same scene, the same spectacle, visible through the blinds, is repeated many times with minute variations, but the suspicions of the jealous husband are never defined. Tragedy is never analyzed as such. It is implicit in the very detached descriptions of the scene and in the distance between the man looking and the spectacle he observes.

There is no trace in *La Jalousie* of Proustian introspection, no trace of the Gidian character-analysis in *L'Immoraliste*, no trace of the metaphysical anguish in Malraux' *La Condition Humaine* or in Sartre's *L'Age de Raison*. The themes of love, of a jealous husband, and of an unfaithful wife are in the book, and yet one is never absolutely sure that they are in the book. Among the literary ancestors of this kind of writing are American novelists, Hemingway, Faulkner, Dos Passos, those introduced to France largely by Sartre and Camus. *La Jalousie* and the other novels of Robbe-Grillet represent a form of purity in the art of fiction where there is no speculation on human motives, where the reasons for our acts and our emotions are beyond our ken. This bareness of Robbe-Grillet's novels is also apparent in abstract painting, in the novels and plays of Beckett, and in the poems of Francis Ponge.

Dans le labyrinthe of 1959, Robbe-Grillet's fourth novel, is more than ever a nightmarish world where it is difficult to distinguish dreams from reality. A soldier wanders about a city after the moment of the city's defeat. He does not succeed in finding the person to whom he wishes to deliver a package he carries about with him. What is made visible to us during the course of the book belongs to a strictly material reality: things, gestures, small events. The title of "labyrinth" is suitable to the wanderings of the soldier along walls, corridors, sidewalks, through doors and snow and night. This dream-like labyrinth was already perceptible in the city of *Les Gommes*, in the island of *Le Voyeur*, and in the bungalow of *La Jalousie*. The novelist places us in a void, where all the ways lead to an impasse, where time is dislocated, where space is altered, where the world is a closed-in site, suitable as a place for man's obsessions to unfold, and where he lives through a truly Kafkaesque experience.

Among the best of the postwar writers, Michel Butor occupies a high place. He is one of those novelists who, by reason of his remarkably-controlled language, and the seriousness of his literary theory, refuses to allow literature to be considered a diversion. He believes that the authentic work of fiction manifests a new way of being, and this is revealed by the form of the novel. New fictional forms may reveal new things in the world, and new relationships between things and people. In speaking of *Finnegans Wake*, Butor points out that for each reader such a work becomes an instrument of intimate self-knowledge. The portrait of himself he would make after reading *Finnegans Wake* or *A la recherche du temps perdu* is different from the self-portrait he would have made before the reading. A great novel can therefore occupy a place at the very heart of our human experience.

The subject matter of Butor's *La Modification* (1957) would be suitable for a conventional psychological novel. A man in Paris takes a train for Rome in order to see his mistress and bring her back with him to Paris. During the trip he changes his mind. His project is no longer valid when he reaches Rome. He has been changed by the places he sees from the train, by his compartment in the train, by Rome where he is going and which preoccupies his thoughts. All of these matters physical and mental become the real characters of the novel which force Léon to alter his decision. The train trip makes him realize that he is in love, not with Cécile, but with Cécile-who-lives-in-Rome. The reasons for Léon's change of heart are complex, but no reader can be sure of the real reason.

This is one of the points of *La Modification*, and indeed of the new novel: it is impossible to reach any specific unalterable truth. Any search for truth of any kind is impeded and even contradicted by our ignorance, by our solitude.

Butor's characters are revealed to us by the places where they live, by those places that oppress them. The hero is quite typically a prisoner. In *L'Emploi du Temps* (1956), Jacques is a prisoner in the town of Bleston for 365 days. In *La Modification*, Léon is a prisoner for twenty hours in the Paris-Rome express. In Butor's first novel, *Passage de Milan* (1954), all the inhabitants of an apartment house are imprisoned there from seven in the evening until seven o'clock in the morning. A specific period of time represents a kind of prison, but the hero, Léon, for example, in the Paris-Rome train, mentally moves back and forth in time. But this mental freedom of time does not permit him to pierce the mystery of Rome.

La Jalousie and *La Modification* differ widely in style and manner, but in common they have traits associated today with the *nouveau roman*. The type of hero, endowed with a civic status and a biography, has disappeared from this new type of novel. A subject matter, based upon a continuous narrative and anecdotes and episodes, has given way to the description of a world where nothing is stable or certain, and where characters, as we know them in the traditional novel, do not exist. The principal character in the *nouveau roman* is no one in particular, but he is a figure whose fantasies and obsessions become a world in themselves, far more real than the world he is looking at. He is an observer, as in *La Modification*, and he becomes so absorbed in his observations that he loses all firm self-identification.

Thus the art of Robbe-Grillet and Butor shows an emptiness, a hollowness at the heart of reality. The new structure of these novels demonstrates this experience of emptiness, of absence. We are never told, for example, that the husband in *La Jalousie* is jealous, but we may feel this by watching him watch his wife standing beside a man. The function of the *vous*, used by Butor in *La Modification* is a form of call or challenge to the reader by which we realize that the language of the novel is that of an inquisition, and the reader is being assumed into the stream of consciousness.

From book to book, the originality of Claude Simon becomes clearer and stronger. In the new art of the French novel, his place is one of the highest. His rather striking resemblance to Faulkner has often been pointed out. *Le Vent* of 1957, is reminiscent of *Absalom, Absalom!* and *L'Herbe* of 1958, calls to mind *As I lay dying*. There are similar stylistic and structural traits in the two writers: long sentences with parentheses, numerous adjectives, a disrupting of chronology. But the fundamental resemblance is in the picture of a universe dominated by fate, where men are powerless in opposing the obscure forces in the world working against them. The symbol of grass growing silently and slowly, is life fulfilling its destiny without man having any control over it. There is, however, a major difference between Faulkner and Claude Simon. The picture of man's defeat in Faulkner is related to a punishment. His is a religious universe where fate means guilt. There is no concept of sin in the world of Claude Simon. The good and the wicked who make up Faulkner's world would have other designations in Simon's world: those clear-minded men who ridicule an absurd world where every human initiative seems grotesque and derisive; and the others (*salauds*, as Sartre would call them) who accept the mechanical routine of history and exploit it for personal benefit.

La Route des Flandres (1961) is one of the most skillfully composed Simon books, in which no one action is uppermost, but where we follow a series of scenes, of pictures, of states of being. No one story or episode is clearly defined. The death of a horse would seem to be an episode of some importance. At any rate, it bears relationship with other developments: with men who are prisoners in Germany, with a jockey's memory of a race, with the owner of a stable. Gradually, by means of minute sketches, a world is composed and we, the readers, become prisoners of this world. We become attached to the admirable concreteness of Swann's world: the bodies of the characters, their gestures, the landscape surrounding them. But it is difficult to become attached to the characters themselves because they do not suffer and do not reveal any particular passion. The novelists of the nineteenth century, Balzac and Dostoevsky, exploited passions, and later with the twentieth-century novelists, Proust, Faulkner and Bernanos, the intense analysis of passion seems to have come to an end. The world has to be reinvented or rediscovered by the new novelists before love in the world can be reinvented, to use the famous phrase of Rimbaud. Butor, Sarraute, and Simon are setting the new décors, and rediscovering objects, wind, and grass. The new novel is not merely a stylistic exercise, a transformation of the fictional genre. It is a discovery of an original freshness in the world.

One of the youngest of the new novelists, J. M. G. Le Clézio, published in 1966 his third book, *Le Déluge*, and it confirmed the promises of his first novel *Le Procès-Verbal* (1963) and his collection of stories *La Fièvre* (1965). The term *école du regard* applies admirably to Le Clézio's art of *Le Déluge* where there is an accumulation of pictures, of conversations overheard, of familiar sensations minutely described, as the hero François Besson walks through the streets of Nice (never named). The inventory of things, streets, houses, does not have the lyric quality of Camus' writing, and it is not expressed with the pure objectivity which characterizes the art of Nathalie Sarraute and Robbe-Grillet. This semi-metaphysical, half-somnolent walker through the city is an intellectualized, gallicized Faulkner or Hemingway character who looks carefully at all the spectacles a city can offer, and pushes this experience of observation to its ultimate consequences of murder, of collapse into death, of "flood."

After Besson's acceptance of the idea of death, at the beginning of the book, his thirteen days wandering through the city is the verification of this idea, because he finds the representation of death everywhere. During the walk, which resembles at times Bloom's walk through Dublin, and at other times a pastiche of calvary, the protagonist discards, one after the other, the various reasons for which a man lives: family, work, love, food. The labyrinthine aspect of the city is infernal, and each episode vaguely resembles a circle of hell, a stage in a gradual descent. The power of the book is the sentiment of anguish that comes from the spectacle of the most commonplace scenes. It is another example of the metaphysical anguish of being, which—since the novels of Sartre, Camus, and Beckett—is the principal problem exposed in a variety of ways in the French novel from 1950 on. It is to be found in the prose poems of Henri Michaux, in the theatre of the absurd (Ionesco, Adamov, Arrabal), in the new paintings (Georges Mathieu) and sculptures (Richier).

Le Clézio's protagonist is mesmerized by the real world, and he becomes, during the action of the story, the prey of this reality, its victim. He feels wounded and mutilated by everyone who looks at him and speaks to him. He feels himself gradually being changed by them. He watches his own metamorphosis taking place, as he turns into something monstrous, something inhuman. Everything he looks at becomes a parody, and everyone he speaks to becomes a false prophet. He tries to escape from this world he sees in his hallucination, but he is trapped by it, compressed by it. His last willful action, that of letting his eyes be burned by the sun, is the logical consequence of his being too dazzled by the world. *Le Déluge* could be called by the last words said by Fontenelle as he was dying: "the difficulty of being." Its moral theme comes from the oldest myth in literature, that of the quest, the seeking through space for some god and some answer. In this sense, Besson is a contemporary Jason and Tristan, a Ulysses seeking some improbable solution, some unmanageable return. No trace and no rest is possible in such a walk as this.

No literary form reflects more accurately than does the novel, the ever-changing structure of society and the ever-changing moral and metaphysical problems of society. During the period between the two wars (*l'entre-deux-guerres*), novelists were less interested in telling a story than in raising questions in the minds of their readers: moral problems in the novels in Mauriac (*Le Désert de l'Amour*) and Montherlant (*Les Céli-bataires*), general metaphysical problems concerning the meaning of life, as in Malraux (*La Condition Humaine*), theological problems concerning man's destiny and salvation, as in Bernanos (*Sous le soleil de Satan*) and Julien Green (*Léviathan*). With World War II and the advent of the existentialist writers, there was a fairly distinct break with those two types of novels: the novel where the story element is strong (Zola, Bourget, Anatole France), and the novel with a moral-metaphysical preoccupation. *La Nausée* and *L'Etranger* are not narratives in the usual sense. They are addressed to the conscience of the reader rather than to his understanding of traditional morality and theology. They start all over again, in the history of man's thought, by asking the reader to examine the reason for man's existence and for his actions. The existentialist novel shows man facing the strangeness of his life and of his habits, experiencing disgust with himself and with his existence, becoming aware of a fundamental absurdity in his behavior, in the seeming falseness in his earlier religions and philosophies.

Then came, in the fifties, the so-called new novel, which grew out of the remains of the existentialist novel. By the time the Fifth Republic was created, the French novelist had become, especially with the example of Alain Robbe-Grillet, a technocrat of the novel, whose art seems to be a minute inventory of objects, a form that has cut itself off totally from the routine of the psychological novel. The new novelists have not found suitable for their books the great social-political themes of *War and Peace*, the personal psychological problems of *A la recherche du temps perdu*, the theological theme of man's salvation of *Journal d'un curé de campagne*.

What do they write about, then? What is left for them to write about? When asked this question, they have almost all answered—"about nothing!" Their subject matter is quite deliberately reduced to a minimum. *Le Planétarium* of Nathalie Sarraute is about the purchase of some chairs and an exchange of apartments. *Le Square* of Marguerite Duras is a conversation between a man and a woman sitting on a public bench. *Le Dîner en Ville* of Claude Mauriac is a long rather futile conversation around a dinner table in Paris. *La Modification* of Butor centers on the problem of whether a man in a train between Paris and Rome should break off or not break off his liaison with his Roman mistress. There is no trace of social or political commitment in these books, but there is often a formal pattern of setting, elaborately described: the plan of a city, for example, in Butor's *L'Emploi du Temps*, or the seating plan of a dinner table in *Le Dîner en Ville*.

The theory of commitment, so significant in existentialist writing of the forties, is replaced by the problem of perception in the new novels of the fifties and sixties. The differences between these writers are evident in the various ways they approach the problem of perception, in the degrees they manifest of awareness of the exterior world, and the degrees of their grasp of the inner reality of the mind. Whereas the characters of Robbe-Grillet analyze perceptions without revealing any emotion, those of Butor do reveal some degree of emotion.

One of the most difficult and perceptive of the new French writers, Jean-Pierre Faye, has quite succinctly expressed his aim in writing, as a search for a new expression of the reality of beings. He looks upon the traditional psychological language as a kind of code which corresponds to very little today. The psychology of his characters will be revealed by the description of their exterior behavior, by the expressions on their faces, by their gestures.

M. Faye today lives in the apartment once occupied by André Gide, on the rue Vaneau, which is on the frontier of a neighborhood in Paris very much associated with the new writing in France, with the experimental revolutionary movement in all the arts today, —that defiant arrogant little island of Saint-Germain-des-Prés. Ever since the days in the forties when Jean-Paul Sartre and Mme Simone de Beauvoir were actually visible writing at their tables in the Flore and the Deux-Magots, and Picasso was visible across the street in his favorite restaurant of La Brasserie Lipp, Saint-Germain has grown into a citadel protecting the new theorists and the new exponents of the novel.

During the earlier generation, the two novelists whose work seems today to represent the starting point for the new writing, the real literary ancestors whose books are always taken into account in any estimate of today's accomplishments, lived just to the northwest and the northeast of Saint-Germain: Proust, in the Eighth Arrondissement, and Joyce in Montparnasse. With Proust, the novel ceased being a description of the world and the inhabitants of the world, in order to become another kind of description involved with the leading questions of what the world is and what man is. The novel in the new form given to it by Beckett, Faye, and Le Clézio, does not represent an effort to dehumanize literature and suppress it, but rather to adapt it to today's world. Rather than describe those psychological motifs that are easily recognizable, the novelist prefers to seize motivations, attractions, repulsions as they occur in their most elementary stage in their characters.

During the period before World War II, the novel had been enriched by the work of three or four giants: by Joyce, who attempted to narrate the entire human experience of a few characters; by Proust, who described a world of characters and their environment; by Faulkner, who narrated the history of entire families; by Henry Miller, who wrote an unusually vibrant narrative of confession. By comparison with these books, the world of Beckett's disinherited characters, and of Sarraute's anti-novel, seems a radically changed form of fiction. Of all the experimentalists today, Samuel Beckett goes farthest in his determination to abolish strict frontiers between types of writing. His novels are a medley of confessions, dreams, humorous anecdotes, revolting episodes. He succeeds more than the others in raising the curtain that separates him from reality and that keeps him from seeing himself. He has quite literally shattered the form, the setting of the novel.

Objects are used by Balzac and Flaubert in the descriptions of the exterior world in their novels, and they are usually objects owned by the character and serve, therefore, a social function. They signify material, social, or moral values. Such meanings are not assigned by Robbe-Grillet to objects in his novels. He avoids all historical and moral implications that are so important in the novel of psychological and social analysis.

The successful French novelists of fifteen or twenty years ago, a Julien Green, for example, and a François Mauriac, have tended today to give up the writing of novels for the writing of essays and personal journals. As the psychological novel has disappeared, the personal essay has proliferated. Even Sartre, with *Les Mots*, has published a kind of autobiography. To the new novel, whose audience is limited, should be added, in all justice, certain forms of writing for the movies, and radio and television, forms that are often close to fiction, and that reach very wide audiences.

The youthful heroes and the stern matriarchs in the novels of Green and Mauriac have been replaced by a nondescript hero who looks at the world through a keyhole or a blind, who is often suspected of crimes but whose action is never clear, who keeps close to the walls lining the sidewalks as he crosses the city, who is obsessed by the details of objects, such as an ashtray on a café table or a pinball machine, who is often nameless like the characters of Kafka, who follows not the exterior sequence of events, but the chaotic and muddled memories that live on in his mind, memories that relate him to the past and convert his present into his past.

The German Novel
In the Wake of Organized Madness

SIEGFRIED MANDEL

In the serious German novel after World War II, one finds no heroes of any traditional stamp and very little of heroism. The literary landscape is heavily overcast by disillusionment; isolated figures—outcasts, outsiders, value-seekers, ruminators, freaks, and other flotsam—wander between present and past in search of certainty, truth, values, happiness, and redemptive signs that would invest the designation "man" with dignity and meaning even amid the seemingly senseless and terrible unpredictability of history. Art feeds on life, and if life is corrupted, the novel—as it does in German fiction—will reflect it unsparingly and the novelist will react to it with a perception that burns more deeply than that of the historian. The roots of the unheroic in German fiction are traceable indeed to fact. The metamorphosis of fact into the larger reality of the novel is a task which German novelists have set themselves with almost unprecedented vigor. What is the unheroic, raw data?

Germany's corrosive social, cultural, and political crises go back to the twenties which were scarred by disastrous inflation and rising nationalistic hysteria and neurotic politics, particularly in response to the Treaty of Versailles. Scapegoats and panaceas were avidly sought, allowing National Socialism to capitalize on discontent and fantasy. If the average man, not unexpectedly, was deluded into believing that the Third Reich would solve his problems and at the same time restore Germany to glory, how much more culpable were the intellectual and academic "Heil" shouters and book-burners. Martin Heidegger, for instance, a philosopher of considerable reputation, enjoined the German "Volk" to vote for the Führer "who does not beg for votes" but affords the nation "an opportunity for self-directed existence" (Dasein). More than willfully espousing totalitarianism, Heidegger, among many, prostituted the language of philosophy to the most obscene form of politics.

The perversion of language coursing through mass media after 1932 was rapid. Not only did it consist of the most colloquial gutter vilification of so-called non-Aryans but it used traditional forms in new contexts: Hitler's cohorts become "apostles," *Mein Kampf* was called the "sacred book of National Socialism," Nazism was the "miracle of belief" in the "justice" of the Führer or "savior;" "right is what benefits the nation." How easily the "little" man adjusted to the new context is clear in the postwar novels. Language, with its emotional and evocative power, was at the mercy of its ruthless users, and had to be thoroughly burnished after the demise of the Third Reich. An extraordinary group of poets—among them Ingeborg Bachmann, Paul Celan, Günter Eich, Peter Huchel—led the way for the novelists.

After the war in lectures to his countrymen on *Die Schuldfrage, The Question of German Guilt,* the distinguished philosopher Karl Jaspers saw a critical need for "learning to talk to one another" openly. But his advice for a steady series of cleansing dialogues was largely wasted, except upon writers who were to explore the terrain mapped out by Jaspers. He reasoned that moral guilt or crime charged to a whole people is nonsense because "the criminal is always an individual." Further, he claimed that the collectivist, racial, and nationalist ideas held by a majority of Germans was drilled into their heads by Nazism. While Jaspers' first premise is justified by its recognition of personal responsibility, the second premise too conveniently put aside former German endorsement of ideas of national purpose, the self-directed national and collective existence, and the unity of "Volk" myth, and the cheering of army conquests. Clarifying the meaning of German guilt, Jaspers suggested several categories: political guilt—the answering for acts of the régime which people tolerated; moral guilt—giving support and cooperation to the régime; metaphysical guilt—standing by while crimes were committed.

Not only was Germany a prison after 1933 but external events served to keep it so, according to Jaspers: in 1933, the Vatican signed a concordat enormously prestigious to Hitler; all nations recognized Hitler; admiring voices were heard, including Churchill's; in 1935, England signed a naval pact with Hitler; in 1936, Hitler occupied the Rhineland, unopposed by France; and in the same year foreigners flocked to Berlin for the Olympic Games, as oblivious as most Germans to events; in 1939, Russia made its unconscionable pact with Hitler. Symbolically these unheroic and morally blind times were climaxed in 1938 by Chamberlain's umbrella and the swastika at Munich, a city where National Socialism had its birth.

That no outsiders helped to save the Germans from themselves was the lament of liberals within their prison. Yet within, the picture was even more grim and unheroic. If the functionaries of universities and church institutions were preoccupied with saving their skins and bricks and mortar, how else could the majority act in the absence of moral example? Survival pretexts and evasion were the main order of the day. Cardinal Faulhaber, archbishop of Munich, tried to fend off Nazi threats against Catholicism by denying divine inspiration to Jewish holy books and distinguishing between modern Jews and those before Christ, a view no less subtle than the consistent anti-Semitism preached by journals close to Vatican thinking and steadily infesting middle-class views. Protestantism was divided, with the Thuringian Christians attempting to twist Lutheranism toward Nazism while a group of ministers led by theologians Karl Barth and Pastor Martin Niemöller (shunted off into a concentration camp) courageously resisted such tactics. Arrests of hundreds of clergymen served to justify the cooperative ones and to subdue the others. When in 1938, upon a Nazi signal, synagogues went up in flames during the "Crystal Night" all over Germany and German-dominated territories, there was pathetic silence and public paralysis. Written in the wind was the warning that eventually all churches would be doomed, but few read the message.

A search for heroes and martyrs among literary figures would be almost equally futile. Those who sensed the Nazi contempt for man as no more than raw material to serve the will of a totalitarian state felt personal danger; even more they hoped to preserve the artistic achievements of their generation somehow and made the often painful choice of emigrating: Thomas and Heinrich Mann, Stefan George, Franz Werfel, Bertolt Brecht, Alfred Döblin, Stefan and Arnold Zweig, George Kaiser, Carl Zuckmayer, Anna Seghers, Ernst Toller, and a host of others well known to the German public. George and Mann were the most distinct propaganda losses to the new regime. The incarceration of Ernst Wiechert in 1938 showed the wisdom and proved the necessity for the emigration. Gerhart Hauptmann, Ernst Jünger, and Gottfried Benn put on blindfolds which they never removed. Their activity was called by the charitable name of inner emigration. Jünger and Benn eventually joined the Army, hoping to find purer air. The fact that the "Wehrmacht" had changed from pre-Nazi times never appeared in their writings. Abandoned was the Prussian code of military law containing the critical clause which emphasized that orders issued with criminal content were not to be obeyed, and that soldiers obeying such orders would themselves be liable to punishment. To the absence of this clause one might well attribute the total savagery visited upon Europe by the Nazi machine and the Wehrmacht: 6 million Jews, 6 million Poles, 17 million Russians (including military), 30,000 French hostages alone, countless Czechs, Greeks, and other Europeans. If one adds to the picture the death camps and portable extermination units, the medical experiments, the genocide programs, the deliberate plowing under and obliteration of towns and people, the mind boggles and the imagination staggers. If Germans point out that much of their young generation had been cut down in their youth and that one-and-a-half million civilians perished during air attacks alone, particularly in Dresden —that too is part of the picture of terror and counter-terror. Literature was to have no dearth of facts, issues, and problems to draw upon.

By consensus of German historians, critics, and writers, 1945—the year of defeat—was called "Das Jahr Null," loosely translated as the zero point, implying a new starting point. Yet historically and symbolically, Germany as a pariah nation could fall no lower. Culturally the years from 1932 to 1945 had been rendered sterile by the absence of moral values; yet, hopes were high that the notable literary group which had gone into exile would provide a drive toward rejuvenation. For many reasons, this proved to be a false hope. Although the outside world regarded the authors in exile as representative of the German cultural genius and as a force which would inspire the young generation and revive older tradition, the German reading public curiously enough was disinclined to throw bridges over the gulf which slowly had been created between themselves and the authors in exile. The feeling was that they belonged to a literary period of the past, that some of their writing was antiquated and no longer spoke of the problems which the Germans faced, that their judgments were too bitter, and that they really did not "belong" any more. This was made clear to a number of returnees, particularly Alfred Döblin.

Apparently the National Socialist indoctrinations through mass media, popular literature, and educational channels—from grade school through the university—had their appalling effect. The absence of countervailing literature and the absence of liberal education seem to have induced intellectual lethargy and one-sidedness, and at worst hostility to anything and anyone not German. Ironically, some of the persecutors readily assumed a persecution complex, and for perhaps a decade after the war much of the German population could not bear to face its own immediate past and tried to turn away from the bright glare of exposure that was being cast on that period of its history. For many years after 1945, it was noticeable that non-fiction which dealt with the past—and the more remote the better—dominated the reading market. Obviously, much that was written could be termed escape literature.

Although it was possible to avoid confrontation with the Hitler years—variously called unresolved, undigested, indigestible, events did not permit the same luxury in regard to immediacies. Cold, hunger, and general misery plagued the big cities; the problem of returning soldiers began to swell; a year-long blockade of Berlin started by the Russians in 1948 was broken by the Allies, but the Berlin crisis remained, symbolized by the *de facto* partition into a West and a Soviet-dominated East Germany. In 1949, the Federal Republic and the Democratic Republic were formed, signalizing two Germanies and two socio-political and economic structures. At the same time, the currency reform and a frenetic work drive which engaged West Germans' energies and frustrations led to the "economic miracle" which made it dubious as to who were the victors in Europe. A workers' revolt in 1953 was sparked in East Berlin, but the drive for political freedom was crushed. In 1960, anti-Semitic manifestations became punishable by law for the first time in the history of cyclical German anti-Semitism and at a time when only a handful of survivors had remained. Then with a hateful and retributive gesture, East Germany in 1961 put up the Berlin wall to sunder the city; and in 1962, undercover actions by the West German Chancellery to silence journalistic exposés, resulting in the *Spiegel* affair, gave many the uneasy impression that democratic processes were still not entirely operative.

All these raw data of the past and present—overcast by the cold war—became grist for the novelists' mill, matters for sober and sombre assessment, and matters for conscience. The variety of ways in which conscience became manifest through literary form is a main reward in the study of the German postwar novel. Unlike philosophy, poetry, and drama, the German novel itself has had very little continuity of development. Since the Renaissance, the German novel essentially has had to depend upon the talents of clusters of novelists who broke trails without leading to main avenues. Much the same may be observed today. Novelists drew their literary inspiration less from other novels than from other art forms.

Without taking a detour, we might point to the dramatic writing of Wolfgang Borchert (1921–47), which became the touchstone for other writers. Even his biography had the kind of authenticity which led to a sympathetic hearing, especially the dominant theme of the returning soldiers' plight. Borchert had a number of careers in his short lifetime, including book-selling, acting, and unhappy servitude as soldier. In 1941 he was wounded at the eastern front and some of his disgruntled comments about the National Socialist regime, which he put into letters to his friends, were reported to the authorities by the censor, with the result that he was courtmartialed and assigned to severe front-line duty. He was finally returned to Germany, after having been hospitalized at Smolensk, and gained a furlough. During the furlough he recited his poems in a cabaret; his unflattering remarks again caught the attention of authorities, who incarcerated Borchert and condemned him to death. Saved by the war's end, he started to write furiously. Broken in health, he sought a cure in Switzerland but died in 1947 on the day before his well-known drama *Draussen vor der Tür (The Man Outside)* was performed as a radio play (the "Hörspiel," a social-consciousness genre tried by almost every important novelist—but whose popularity was cut short by television). In his stories and drama Borchert briefly revived expressionistic polemic and pictured the fate of the returning soldier in the darkest possible hues. His people shout at one another in huge, sweeping monologues. They never converse or understand each other: "Give an answer. Why are you silent, why?" Protest against war, private anguish, and obsessive nightmares mark his characters. Barely under control is the language of the returning soldier Beckmann who delivers this vehement monologue:

> There stands a man and plays the xylophone. He plays with a frantic rhythm. And with it he sweats because the man is extraordinarily fat. And he plays on his giant xylophone and because it is so large he must race up and down the side of the xylophone before each stroke. And he sweats because he is in fact very fat. But he sweats no sweat. That is the peculiar thing about it. He sweats blood—steaming dark blood. And the blood runs in two broad, red streams down his pants so that from afar he looks like a general. Like a general! A fat, bloody general. He must be a battle-proven general because he has lost both arms. Yes, he plays with long thin prostheses which look like the grips of hand grenades, hollow and with a metal ring. The general must be a strange musician because the wooden slats of his huge xylophone are not made out of wood. No, believe me . . . they are made of bones.

Beckmann calls up what seem to be millions of grinning skeletons who rise out of mass graves with rotted bandages and bloody uniforms; they swarm out of ruins and forests, maimed and howling. Borchert recreates a veritable hell. What does Beckmann want? He wants to become a human being again but cannot find humans; in the days after the war, he must stand outside the door—literally and figuratively. He feels betrayed by society, by the military, and by God; he challenges some unseen figures or force to come forward and explain the meaning of life and give him reasons for continued existence. Theatrics and anguish are so commingled in the portrait of Beckmann that he becomes not a tragic but a pathetic figure. Though a spokesman for the disillusioned, Borchert possessed a vague optimism: "we are a generation fully expecting a new star, in a new life . . . a new heart . . . a new love, a new laughter, a new God." The sentiment gave voice to the feeling of those born into a world they thought was not of their making.

Borchert's writings typify the merits as well as the excesses of the protest literature of the time. With moral indignation, it ruthlessly exposed the clichés with which the intoxicated elder generation had sent its youth into battle and condemned the grotesquely senseless era since 1932. On the other hand, indignation boiled over into unfocused resentment, myopic treatment of inevitable side-effects of the war, and strong self-pity. Possibly, the raw data reviewed earlier just was too overwhelming to cope with and writers, as much as the public, needed distance and time to digest the monstrous accumulation of facts. Indeed, not until the late fifties do we find anything resembling panoramic vision in the German novel; the short story, however, with its limited range but multitudinous slices-of-life proliferated and was a valuable proving ground for writers.

After the war, German writers were dispersed all over the country. Of the emigres, Arnold Zweig, Anna

Seghers, and Bertolt Brecht decided for idealistic reasons to throw in their lot with East Germany; their productivity suffered and Brecht's encounters with totalitarianism were not happy. Thomas Mann unsuccessfully tried to mediate between East and West but he had no basic sympathy for any contemporaneous German writing. It remained for a group of young people who had made each other's acquaintance as prisoners of war while interned in the United States to band together and upon their return to West Germany to found a journal called *Der Ruf* (*The Call*). Vociferously they demanded complete political and literary reorientation toward the left. When their political imbroglios were thought harmful, the United States Military Government abolished their publication. Nonconformists though they were, their protests had so much in common that they decided on informal ties through the so-called "Group 47," meeting only when they wished. Their political activism abated over the years and the loose confederation of individualists became a principal source of important writers and critics. As a long-standing and belligerent exponent of the ideas of the group, Walter Jens felt that postwar writers had to find their own medium for expressing their experience.

> We say what seems to us to be right; truth we no longer know and no one needs to believe us. Pursued by the horrors of reality, we have lost the possibility of making decisions with perfect freedom.

Starting with perplexity and anger, writers began to look for certainties and values—a search which informed their work and gave a sense of purpose to German postwar fiction. During the first several years after the war, the outlook for German literature looked dim—an almost total vacuum was waiting to be filled. A number of authors returning from exile, like Erich Kästner, began to edit journals which featured pre-Fascist authors and some leading international thinkers whose contributions emphasized socio-logical, political, and philosophical subject matter. Few of these periodicals, which were subsidized either by the American or Soviet power, survived or had much of an impact, except upon a limited readership. On the salutary side, these publications did acquaint German readers with authors and works banned dur-ing the Third Reich, particularly through excerpts from notable writings. Also the names of foreign au-thors were introduced and their works later were to be translated and widely read.

In many respects Heinrich Böll was a follower of Borchert. Not, however, a follower of his apocalyptic outcries or of the Borchert who felt that the present was worth living for and that it was worth loving the "gigantic desert called Germany," loving it as "Chris-tians love their Christ" because of Christ's suffering. In an introduction to Borchert's works, Böll defends Borchert's subjective reactions which were almost dis-dainfully called by critics "Aufschrei" (a crying out). Böll flayed the critics who were not moved by the bitterness of death: "But children cry out, and in the calmness of world history reverberates the death cry of Jesus Christ." He points out that Borchert is the prod-uct of friction between the individual and history and that Borchert's skeletonized man is both frightening and splendid. Borchert could not be indifferent, and in that lay his strength, according to Böll.

Böll, an emancipated Catholic Rhinelander, was born in Cologne in 1917, the son of a cabinetmaker, and was apprenticed early to the book trade. In 1939 he was inducted into the German army, and served on the Russian front where he was wounded; eventually infantry Corporal Böll became a prisoner of war in an American camp in the eastern part of France. After the war he returned to Germanistic studies and at the same time became an apprentice in a carpenter shop;

later he was a city-employed statistician in Cologne. As an outgrowth of his war experiences and the childhood influence of family and several teachers who abhorred Nazism, Böll loathed self-righteousness and machinations among all segments of the population, despised professional clerical careerists, and felt that the disintegration of the past needed not to be prettied up and could not be easily healed or glossed over.

Böll's early short stories, novellas, and novels show the influence of Borchert with his staccato prose-effects, sentimentality, and sensational touches. That his early concern would be for the horror of the war and its aftermath was made clear in a story written in 1947, called *Die Botschaft* (*The Message*): "Then I knew that the war would never be at an end, never, as long as anywhere a wound struck by the war still bled." In the novella *Der Zug war pünktlich* (1949; *The Train was on Time*, 1956), the soldier Andreas has intimations of death and is overwhelmed by Eros and fear.

> Pain sits in his throat and he was never so miserable as now. It is good that I suffer. Because of this I may be forgiven that I sit here in a Lemberg bordello next to an "opera singer" available the entire night for two and a half coupons. . . . and I am glad that I suffer, I'm glad that I almost faint with pain, I am happy because I suffer, suffer insanely, because I may hope that I will be forgiven that I do not pray, pray, only pray and sink to my knees during the last twelve hours before my death. But where can I lie on my knees? Nowhere in the world can I lie on my knees undisturbed.

On the drive to join a frontline unit, the car is machine-gunned, his companions are killed, and the "opera singer" Olina's hand "was hanging over his head through the wreckage of the car and her blood was dripping on his cheeks, and then without his ever knowing it, the tears began to flow from his eyes." Realism as a shortcut to emotional effects persisted for

some time in Böll's work. But even here, Böll gives a
clue to his technique of symbolic contrasts which
forms the ground bass for much of his writing: "Man-
kind is divided into victims and executioners."

In Böll's first novel, *Wo warst du Adam?* (1951;
Adam, where art thou?, 1955) are people from every
walk of life who are either voluntarily or involuntarily
infected by the disease called war. The cue for the
novel is given in a prefatory note taken from the
diaries of Theodor Haecker: "A world catastrophe can
be of great service. It can also serve as an alibi before
God. 'Adam, where art thou?' 'I was in the world
war.' " The varieties of alibis or rationalizations are
illustrated in a series of sketches. Corporal Feinhals
takes refuge in a dream of future happiness with a
Catholic-Jewish girl, Ilona. She however was sent to
an extermination camp where commandant Filskeit, a
passionate lover of choral music and the Death's-Head
Corps, auditioned potential candidates for an inmate
choir. Ilona sang the All-Saints litany "while the face
in front of her shrunk like a terrible excrescence."
Something was touched in Filskeit and he went ber-
serk, gunning down Ilona and ordering a general massacre. Similarly, with the war's end in sight, Corporal
Feinhals' shrapnel-torn body rolls over the threshold
of his home and the narrative abruptly breaks off.
Pointedly the pointlessness of war is made clear as well
as the fact that there were no heroes, only brutal
opportunists, indifferent people, soulful and soulless
ones, and behind them were thousands of "ministers
of death" only too ready with gallows and
tommyguns.

Lower middle-class domestic life absorbed Böll's attention in the novel *Und sagte kein einziges Wort*
(1953; *Acquainted with the Night*, 1954), taking for
his text the lines from a Negro spiritual: ". . . dey
nailed Him to the cross . . . He never said a word."
"Chilled by the dreadful breath of poverty," and beset
by inarticulateness and lethargy, Fred Bogner tempo-

rarily absents himself from home and his wife Kate, but a penurious and pathetic second honeymoon helps to put Fred back on the road home. The contrast between Fred's revulsion from shabbiness and the touching happiness his wife and children can find despite squalor is rendered through separate monologues by Fred and Kate. The depth of their observations and feelings—especially Fred's fear that he might turn Kate's love into something sallow and haggard—gives this fragile novel more tone than structure. The alternation of narrative points of view, which Böll was to exploit more and more, as well as the terseness of language, marks the sharp isolation of characters.

A gripping and compassionate depiction of widowhood, a kind of half-whoredom for many, and attempts to keep broken families together after the war are present with considerable effect in Böll's novel *Haus ohne Hüter* (1954; *Tomorrow and Yesterday*, 1957). A new generation of youngsters are given their perspective on life by a parade of euphemistic "uncles" and confused mothers so that Nella Bach's boy views home, school, and life with a mixture of naïvete and forced precociousness, which remind one of Salinger's novels, two of which Böll translated into German. Nella, whose poet-husband vanished in battle, prefers a succession of uncles and the "unavoidable" to marriage and the possibility of another widowhood. For men she largely has contempt: the warmakers who created "widow factories" with millions of victims, the critics—culture vultures who live on her dead husband's poetry, and priests with their routine massaging of the soul. Two possibilities for fictional drama emerge when Nella makes an assignation with the man responsible for her husband's death and when she receives an offer from a dear friend to rebuild her life. Yet Böll deliberately skirts the dramatic potential in favor of portraying silent suffering. The only one allowed the slightest glimmer of momentary hope is the boy whose memory is not too deeply scarred.

The consistent quality of Böll's work netted him, in 1951, one of the rare awards given by "Group 47" of which he became a member; however, he incurred the displeasure of some critics for rummaging among the ruins (critics called it "Trümmerliteratur"), for spending too much time in the wash-kitchen ("Waschküche"), and for ruffling esthetic sensibilities. Böll countered by saying that material for fiction is not confined to castles or specific milieus and that uppermost in his mind is the picture of two-thirds of humanity in starvation and a world reeking with plunder. For him social and political engagement "is the premise, that is to say, the foundation upon which I build what I understand to be art." Among the literary figures admired by Böll is Charles Dickens who looked into poorhouses, jails, schools, and other institutions, writing about them and finding satisfaction in rousing popular sentiment. He admires the energy and sympathy coursing through Thomas Wolfe's work, and although Böll's own style is worlds apart from Dickens or Wolfe, he tried to emulate their objective. Böll had managed to give the spoken language the dignity of literature. Despite his programmatic aims, he had no illusions: "It is our task to remind people that the human being does not exist in order to be bureaucratically used, and that the disorders of the world are not so superficial and simple that one can heal the world in a few short years." Justifiably, Böll has been called the watchdog and chronicler of the Adenauer era and a "Zeitkritiker," a critic of contemporary events.

Before discussing Böll's major novel—*Billiard um halb zehn* (1959; *Billiards at half-past Nine*, 1962), it is of interest to look at several other statements which clarify his art. Böll notes that the writer's function is "to decipher the actualities in order to obtain the real." He searches for the significant amid the mass of everyday events—the actualities; he arranges the details, and creates a sum or the reality called a novel: "Reality is a message which must be accepted . . . a task which man must solve." Böll is a secular moralist who reacts passionately to what he feels are distortions of religious, political, and social values: "Only one instrument remains for the artist, namely, his conscience; but he has a conscience as a Christian and as an artist, and both these consciences are not always in agreement. The dilemma remains, to be a Christian and at the same time an artist, and yet without being a Christian artist." The strength of individual conviction is pronounced in Böll's work.

Böll regards time as consisting of three erratically-moving discs: time past, present, and a time which might have been or never was except in the imagination or in wishes. Each represents a stratum of experience through direct narration, interior monologues, conversations, and recurring motifs. In *Billiards at half-past Nine,* not until almost the last page do all the pieces fit together to allow the reader to view the over-all story of three generations, the Fähmel family of architects. The patriarch of the family, Heinrich, in 1907 creates a great design for the building of St. Anthony's Abbey during the time of the Kaiser, his son Robert dynamites the abbey during the German retreat at the end of World War II, and his grandson Joseph rebels against what he feels to be a senseless cycle. The cycle of construction, destruction, and reconstruction matches the historical periods covered, symbolically and literally. Whatever action we see is centered within seven hours of Saturday, September 6, 1958: "This was the perpetual present, moved steadily on by the second hand, here today, now . . ." All remembrances and reflections about the past, filtered through the many different minds, give the present its meaning. Throughout the novel the reader is constantly reminded of the inexorable forward movement of time ticked off by the clock as against the unchecked oscillations of the characters' reflections. The clock-time and the calendar fate of St. Anthony's Abbey are the fixed points of reference which hold the unpredictable and far-roaming memory pictures together.

Aside from the cyclical history of the abbey, there is a similar development within the family: the founding of the family, its disruption during the war (one son was killed, another became an indoctrinated Nazi, and the third was a passive victim) and at the end of the novel a family reunion during which hope is placed upon the grandson. The relation which Böll has established between victim and executioner appears again in this novel in the guise of a group called the People of the Lamb and those who advocate the Sacrament of the Buffalo (symbolic for raw power). Irony resides in the fact that the mother, who is mentally unhinged by events, is one of the few persons of unimpeachable integrity. From the vantage point of a sanitarium she reflects upon the supposedly sane world:

All of us here know that all men are brothers, even if they be hostile ones. Some have tasted of the *Host of the Lamb*, only a few of us of the *Host of the Beast*, and my name is *got to get a gun, get a gun,* and my Christian name is *forward with Hindenburg, hurrah.* [The italicized slogans are associated with the patriotic fervor of her two sons.] Forget all your bourgeois prejudices for good, your conversational clichés; here the classless society rules. And stop complaining about losing the war. Good heavens, did you really lose two wars, one after the other? You could have lost seven for all of me. Stop your sniveling, I wouldn't give five cents for all the wars you lost; losing children is worse than losing wars. You can be an altar boy here in the Denklingen Sanitarium, it's a highly respected occupation, and don't make speeches to me about the German future. I read about it in the newspapers: The German future is all pegged out. If you have to weep, don't blubber. So they've been unjust to you, too? Impaired your honor, yes, what's the use of honorableness when any stranger can make dents in it? But now relax, in this booby hatch they take care of you fine, in this place they go into it every time your soul lets out a squeak, all complexes respected here. Just a question of money: if you were poor, it would be cold water and a good thrashing, but here they cater to every one of your whims.

Some of the German critics in 1959 were upset by the outspokenness of Böll's Mother Fähmel who in one of her moments of anger also says,

> Are you all blind? You just don't know any more where you are. I tell you . . . the whole pack of them have partaken of the *Host of the Beast*. Dumb as earth, deaf as a tree, and as terribly harmless as the beast in his last incarnation. Respectable, respectable. I'm scared . . . I've never felt such a stranger among people, not even in 1935 and not in 1942. Maybe I do need time, but even centuries wouldn't be enough to get me used to their faces. Respectable, respectable, without a trace of grief. What's a human being without grief?

Böll does not accept the comfortable partitioning of historical periods in order to divorce the past from the present; each person has his own associative past from which he cannot be absolved. Mother Fähmel is frightened by the things which have not changed: some of the old guard are still around in very respectable official positions. For her the past lives in the present, especially when she sees the indifferent cleric who routinely intoned the Introit over her murdered son. For the mother there is no possibility of reconciliation and after long deliberation she decides to shoot one of the dignitaries who symbolize for her all the professional opportunists and the evil in her world. Her son Robert stands midway between the rocklike decency and urbanity of his father and the derangement of his mother, seeking stability through an unvarying routine of playing billiards. The game is a narcotic to allay the terror of memory. He had dynamited the abbey in a moment of nihilistic compulsion, rationalizing that the *ruins* would provide a more fitting monument for his brother and wife who died needlessly during the war; society's efforts to preserve monuments symbolic of institutions rather than to preserve life seemed intolerable to Robert. But even Robert's routine is not free from the insistent intrusion by a police chief called Nettlinger, previously an informer for the Gestapo and now "a democrat by conviction." Nettlinger is a scathing portrait of the cultivated person whose charming veneer hides the sentimental murderer and who cleverly neutralizes the former victims of his sadism. Because of Robert's conscience even as a young man, he had been "unable to tolerate injustice" and consequently had to become involved in politics whatever the results. Böll seems to find human behavior to be dependent upon the individual's conscience and sense of justice. It may be asked how else it is possible to explain the attitude of an ex-Nazi judge who asserts that had there been a law to kill all people wearing glasses he would have upheld it, as compared with the attitude of many a Scandinavian who sheltered victims of persecution at the risk of his own life because it was the only decent thing to do. Precisely in the rendering of an individual's psychology, not with the historian's analysis of forces or the sociologist's statistics, lies the novelist's strength.

What gives Böll's novel *Billiards at half-past Nine* its dramatic sweep is the slow unthawing of a frozen past, which innundates the present. When this happens, action ensues: negatively, Mother Fähmel shoots at the visible personification of evil; positively, her son Robert gives up his billiards routine and shows signs of stepping back into life.

The sharp criticism and ideas in Böll's next novel *Ansichten eines Clowns* (1963; *The Clown*, 1965) shocked those Germans who felt themselves to be better than the generation of the immediate past; yet the universal applicability of Böll's views ought not to be overlooked. The novel also infuriated some East German officials who saw their bureaucratic structure mercilessly lampooned in one of the incidents, (and who promptly made sure that Böll's work could only be obtained through underground means). Böll's capacity for mordant wit, used sparingly until this novel, now explodes on every page; it is a wit both polished and needle-deft, verging on polemic, and it is turned

against social, political, cultural, and religious pretend-
ers. Instead of the polyphonic structure of *Billiards,*
we have an intense concentration on the near-pica-
resque figure of the professional clown Hans Schnier
who reminds one of the roller-coasting Herzog of Saul
Bellow's novel. If Hans Schnier's ego-baring confessions are disjointed, they reflect the unanchored wandering of his mind and an attempt to regain the contact he has lost with his wife, family, and friends.
Schnier's bitterness is measured by the indictment: "If
our age deserves a name, it must be called the age of
prostitution." Schnier refuses to play the "adjustment" game. He rejects his natural social advantages
as an industrialist's son and is unable to forgive persons their sundry immoralities during the Third Reich
even when they ask him for "secular absolution."
Being honest and being a clown are double liabilities
in a conflict with persons protected by institutions and
convention; no one takes Schnier seriously and this
seems further justified when his gestures become increasingly stupified by alcohol and futility. Like other
Böll creations, Schnier as the lonely man of decent
instinct is no match for the opposition, except ver-
bally. When after a lag of years, Schnier phones his
mother—formerly a rabid war supporter, she automat-
ically answers: "Central Committee of the Societies
for the Reconciliation of Racial Differences." The
past wells up, he remembers her bigoted slogans, and
he impulsively shoots back, "I am a delegate of the
Central Committee of Jewish Yankees, just passing
through—may I please speak to your daughter?" That
the daughter has been sent to her death as a war
volunteer by the mother twists the remark into a ma-
cabre joke. Yet verbal triumphs win no battles as
Schnier knows, nor does skepticism win friends.

Throughout his work, Böll regards life as a sacrament (religious symbolism abounds in the stories and
novels) and deplores the lack of moral power and
persuasion within the political and religious Establish-

ment. Discernible is a progression from realistic sentimentality to fine-veined sentiment, controlled irony,
and narrative strength without which no novelist—no
matter how moralistic—would have an audience.

Liberality of spirit is not always the hallmark of the
creative talent in the twentieth century. Xenophobia,
racial and economic balderdash, elitism and snobbism
infest the work of Eliot and Pound; a dark, mystic
folk-and-soil mythology (and not to speak of the flat-
tery accorded by the German reading public)
prompted Knut Hamsun to proclaim himself a disciple of Hitler; the voluntary capitulation to Nazi barba-
rism by Jean Giono ("I would rather be a live German
than a dead Frenchman") and Henri Montherlant
speak of intellectual corrosion. Moral blindness is confined to no nationality. Of modern German writers,
Gerhart Hauptmann, Gottfried Benn, and Ernst
Jünger broke faith with those readers who believed in
the integrity and moral values of literature. They were
culpable not so much in what they did write but in
what they omitted in their writings even after the
war.
    Intellectualized non-resistance to tyranny, the regret
that modern war is no longer a jousting matter, and
that modern civilization is in a state of decay are ideas
that mark the work and the man Jünger. In 1919, the
24-year-old ex-soldier's diary-document *In Stahlgewit-
tern* (*The Storm of Steel*) meticulously recorded
World War I carnage from the viewpoint of the German "princes of the trenches, brave to madness, with
bloodthirsty nerves" as they shrilly met the enemy and
gave no mercy. It was, in Jünger's eyes, a good sporting
spectacle, "an incomparable schooling of the heart,"
from which he emerged with twenty wounds and
prized decorations. In an untranslated World War II
diary we find an entry describing officer Jünger hold-
ing a glass of burgundy with floating strawberries and

coolly observing from the rooftop of a hotel in occupied Paris an Allied air-strike during an esthetic sunset.

Prussian war mythomania, a refined estheticism that leaned toward the culture of the Renaissance, and a supremely detached view of life characterize Jünger. Paradoxically, he could write a novel *Auf den Marmorklippen* (1939; *On the Marble Cliffs*, 1947), that has been interpreted as ingeniously veiled criticism of Nazism as an unsporting destroyer of civilization, and then write a tract called "The Peace," in which he saw virtue in Nazi conquests as a prelude to necessary European federation and lasting peace. After 1945, he turned to semi-sociological studies. From these preoccupations has grown a style of writing and observation marked by crystalline hardness and fastidious mannerism.

Most of these traits and ideas also are luminously woven into his novel *Gläserne Bienen* (1957; *The Glass Bees*, 1960), which picks up the Spenglerian tune of "modern civilization is doomed." Captain Richard, a discharged cavalryman, has such pessimistic feelings as he is introduced to the industrialist dictator Zapparoni who—like so many of his kind—has successfully projected a saintlike image of himself to the outside world.

The allegorical novel focuses on the span of an afternoon when job-applicant Richard is put to a severe test of courage, mental stamina and sense of social responsibility in Zapparoni's mysterious garden. It ominously swarms with glass bees, the latest marvels of miniaturized technology—micro-robots—that, if mobilized, would constitute the most lethal of advanced weapons. Richard's intellectualized nonresistance to Zapparoni's iron-will may be appalling, but the author makes it starkly plausible. In scenes as harrowing and thought-disturbing as any created by Karel Čapek, George Orwell, or Aldous Huxley, he contributes not only to prophetic and nihilistic literature but also to an understanding of the inner and outer forces that shape many a man's attitude toward tyranny.

A severe dissociation between culture consciousness and humaneness explains the path of Gerd Gaiser (and that of Benn and Jünger) toward a snobbistic illiberality. Literary refinement does much to disguise the tendency, but nevertheless it exists in Gaiser's work. Largely through the type of allegory of which Jünger was fond—a means of putting distance between the crass and the sublime, Gaiser's central ideas take shape: man is at the mercy of fate or impersonal forces; the new technology and technocracy are destructive of elite aspirations; the wounded spirit finds solace in the naturalness of nature rather than the artifice of cities; the lesson of life is learned by observing nature; society is divided into the mob (who play almost no role in Gaiser's works), the materialistic and unimaginative middle class, and the lonely, enduring elite. A line may be charted in his life from patriotic optimism to philosophical pessimism, from concern with the actual to the creation of a mythical Eden, a dreamworld somewhere between life and death.

The son of a vicar, Gaiser was born in 1908 in Würtemberg. He cut short his theological studies and turned from Evangelism to painting and art history, writing his dissertation on Renaissance and early Baroque art. With the outbreak of the war, art-teacher and glider sportsman Gaiser joined the German Air Force and rose to the rank of combat officer. His ardent belief in the German cause resulted in 1941 in some published (*Reiter am Himmel, Riders in the Sky*) and unpublished verse which retrospectively he called "the unripe pieces of a novice without influence." But he flirted with power concepts and extolled the German "masters" and their tasks of destroying and reconstructing the world into a new order, a fanatic political conviction which did not, however, survive the defeat intact; some of the ideas lingered on under the rubric of honor, duty, the good old days, and subtle forms of racism as well as Hamsunite blood-and-soil mysticism. Gaiser's postwar disgruntled neutralism has its fascination because it represents Gaiser's generation, the strongest supporters and victims of the Third Reich. A corps of critics (Günter Blöcker, Curt Hohoff, Hans Egan Holthusen) place Gaiser among the top contemporary German novelists while others (Walter Jens, Helmut Kreuzer, and Marcel Reich-Ranicki) concede his talent, but point to Gaiser's devaluation of man, his depersonalization of the individual, and his disturbing anti-social undertones.

Writing came less easy to Gaiser than painting: "Writing consumes." One can see the literary effort and uneven results in Gaiser's numerous short stories and in his first novel *Eine Stimme hebt an* (1950; *A Voice is Raised*) which brought into being a set of characters and incidents that recur in the later novels. Although at the center of the novel there appears the "Heimkehrer" or the homecoming soldier, Gaiser's approach to the familiar figure in the literature of the twenties and the forties is totally different; he breaks sharply with the realistic art of Borchert and Böll and his characters are less communicative. Gaiser's soldier Oberstelehn, numbed by his wife's unfaithfulness, retreats to his boyhood village where in contact with nature and the example of women who do keep faith, he slowly works his way from apathy to moribund acceptance of the conciliatory idea that "without evil there cannot be the good." The narrative thread is slender as Gaiser relies on moody description of a man's physical and intuitive affinities with nature: birth, battle, defeat—dignity through resistance. One of the set dialogues between Oberstelehn and an apothecary holds interest. The latter has contempt for history that boasts the ascendency of technology over man, a technology which exterminated minorities and subjugated whole nations, a technology capable of chemically reorienting mind and will; man is passé, values are in disorder. Oberstelehn characterizes this as the old-fashioned notion that "the air belongs to the birds" and not to man. Man, he feels, has no kamikaze instinct; he has an inflexible will to survive and to view the future as boundless. The apothecary dubs the ex-soldier as "Mann des Inskünftigen," a man of the future; but in the present, the mob ("Gesindel," a favorite Gaiser term of contempt for the lower classes) tramples decency and honor and does not appreciate the man who seeks order; the mob hounds him out of town. The unclearness of what Gaiser means by "order" has led some critics to detect nostalgia for the Third Reich. We meet Oberstelehn and his principles again in Gaiser's works.

Among the few German novels touching on the air war, Gaiser's *Die sterbende Jagd* (1953; *The Last Squadron*, 1956), has been regarded as the best pictorial and psychological rendering of the warriors of the sky. Like the French novelist Saint-Exupéry, Gaiser is able to capture the special tempo and reflective experience of pilots in their cockpit loneliness, the thunder of battle (the German word "Schlacht," denoting butchery is more apt), and the rationale which permits a German fighter squadron stationed in Norway to persist in a hopeless cause. Often the alternation of regional dialect and compositional passages which aspire to lyricism produce styles in conflict with one another. More successful is Gaiser's merging of the actual and the symbolic exemplified by a scene in which a diving and screaming plane becomes one with the earth. Nature—in the Gaiser canon—is primal and indifferent and within the biological arena man lives his span no matter what he does. Some of Gaiser's pilots submit to orders with resignation and a sense of duty while others participate because they like to fight: "war merely brings out what already exists internally." Barbarities visited upon civilians are somewhat cynically glossed over with the observation that men like to kill when they are given the opportunity and free rein. Gaiser puts Jaspers' categories of individual guilt in still another way: To fight for a cause of which one is convinced is magnificent; not to fight for it, despite conviction, is contemptible; not to espouse a cause and refusal to fight imposes a terrible burden but affords inner peace; to deny a cause and yet to fight for it results in defeat one way or the other. Gaiser implies that action and bravery in themselves are forms of self-assertions in the teeth of obliterating history; his failure, however, to deal with responsibility and the morality of action lends his treatment of guilt a nihilistic air. One might accept Gaiser's possibility of choices as universals, but one also notes that Gaiser and his pilots shifted their views not because of conscience but because of military defeat; conveniently, blame was shifted to the devil Hitler "sent by God, and sent to corrupt us." Only at the point of death does a captain curse those who caused the plague. When the hunters of the sky become the hunted and jousting is eliminated, the hunt dies: "Victory is magnificent for whoever may win." Deprived of victory, what has the homecoming warrior to look forward to in peace time? One of Gaiser's large cast of unheroic characters sees peace as bringing preferment lists, lies, bureaucracy, bribery, commission businesses, and a community spirit dedicated to the elevation of self and the destruction of others; the beneficial potential of peace is passed over in near silence and no indictment is made of the Third Reich as the soldier apparently heeds the injunction: "Don't retain much memory. Don't carry too much with you."

At the end of *Eine Stimme hebt an*, Oberstelehn mysteriously hints that he must go to the mountain, and we guess that he is after further revelations. Gaiser's next novel *Das Schiff im Berg* (1955; *The Ship in*

the Mountain), containing some of his best descriptive prose, is a cosmological fable about a mountain, personifying nature, and the parasitic attempt of a community to lure tourists by commercializing newly discovered natural caves and tunnels. The idea of history and progress, declares Gaiser, is a swindle; the lesson which the temperamental mountain teaches is that man is subject to and inferior to nature, and that for him to attempt to disprove this is to invite catastrophe. That the mountain serves as God's warning to man forms part of Gaiser's belief in the existence of God; man is responsible for the distance between himself and God. Gaiser's chilling primitivism and austere concept of God is further evident when he extols a community Führer, as he had done in his poetry in 1941, who with power inherited from the gods brings order to the life of the animal-like masses. After garnering these revelations, Gaiser descended from the mountain into the city, a composite he calls Neu-Spuhl.

Time has passed and the years have brought prosperity through reconstruction and the economic miracle. Have people changed? In the novel *Schlussball* (1958; *The Final Ball*, 1960), it is obvious that Gaiser thinks not. In fact, the dire prognostication of what peace would bring has been fulfilled. The crass community pictured in *Eine Stimme hebt an* has grown more crass and the widows of the warriors opaquely characterized in *The Last Squadron* suffer even more, while the ex-soldier Soldner (with a Gaiserian halo that has serious blemishes) has a rough time. The subtitle of the novel, "From the beautiful days of the West German city Neu-Spuhl," is entirely ironic and symbolic. Nothing really is "new" and the word Spuhl is associated with a dirty puddle (Pfuhl) in which life breeds and dies as part of the biological cycle.

With considerable skill, Gaiser has adapted modern fictional techniques (a departure for him). Interior monologues, criss-crossings of memory, drastic time-shifts, montages, multiple perspective are put to work effectively and suspensefully to tell us why there were "two dead bodies toward morning." Yet, at the outset, Gaiser warns us that there is little plot. And he is right. The novel develops its intensity through ingeniously delayed resolutions and through slowly unfolding case histories that eventually produce a patterned whole. Capping the school year is a prom which becomes a communal and ritual meeting ground for the citizens of Neu-Spuhl: Soldner, a teacher who stayed in the city to pursue an inept courtship of the widow Herse Andernoth—a courtship complicated by her daughter Diemut's adolescent crush on Soldner; Frau Rakitsch, a businesswoman who deals in pornography, and her son who insanely woos Diemut; the newly-rich Tatzen-Förckh and his wife (who appeared as struggling young people in *Eine Stimme hebt an*); Ditta, a confidante of Diemut; and spooky voices of the dead who hover about the living. Climactic in the novel are the suicide of the wealthy Frau Tatzen-Förckh who in the eyes of neighbors led an enviable life, and the death of Rakitsch who assaults Herse, mistaking her for Diemut, and is pushed backward, to be impaled upon an iron gate.

On the surface we see a novel rich in varieties of experience and emotion, in verbal tonality and atonality, in the play of themes sounded, iterated, and developed. Below the surface, however, seethe ideas—the older hobby horses of Gaiser—not free from sulfurous misanthropy and nihilism. Neu-Spuhl may appear to the casual eye as an ordinary industrial city but to Gaiser it is an eruption upon the earth, choking off nature and cutting off the moon; the terrain is defaced by houses and mechanized transportation. Soldner viewing the city is overwhelmed by an "ailing, irrational lament," but he is consoled by a vision of "the time when the entire spook will be swept away and swallowed up; then nothing will remain of Neu-Spuhl except a discoloration of the earth." Even more dramatic is the novelist's complaint about the lack of human contact with nature as he observes that blood absorbed by the earth is a tolerable thought but smeared on asphalt it becomes unbearable. The mystique of nature, blood, soil, is the undercurrent of the novel. When one talks of decadence, the picture of a profligate Rome of old comes to mind, yet in Gaiser's ultra-conservative view Neu-Spuhl, with its hustle-bustle commercialism and observance of latest fashions in dress and hairdo, seems no different.

If the city is decadent so are most of its citizens. Herr Tatzen-Förckh's ugly name (Tatze signifies claw) mirrors his activity as an insatiable entrepreneur. Predatory too are Frau Rakitsch and her son who variously is described as a mad dog, a spider, a reptile—ingratiatingly subtle but poisonous. This dark-souled and dark-complexioned gypsy and Slavic type pursues the blonde Diemut (close to the word Demut, humility), whose virtue is symbolized by an old-fashioned pigtail. (When Rakitsch dies violently, Gaiser notes that "everyone agreed that this time, truly, the victim was guilty," offering the limpest possible apology to the victims of the Führer poetized by Gaiser.) Although Gaiser doctored up Rakitsch's origin in various editions of the novel, not only are the cartoons of the Third Reich unmistakably reproduced but Gaiser's xenophobia is carried over from his poems and stories, in which the German "blond and white" Volk are superior to foreign nationalities and races. Gaiser hardly runs out of derogatory synonyms for the citizenry and their offspring—mechanical, greedy people, soulless, living only for money and frivolities. Even the solid burgher virtues of thrift—perhaps even the victors who made it possible—are sneered at in a peculiar way as Ditta's mother says, "One must not talk about it, Ditta, but yet our dear God has let us win the war . . . you must not be wasteful; learn how money is made."

There are a minority, however, who exemplify

Gaiserian values. Frau Förckh commits suicide because the closeness to her husband that she enjoyed
during the bitter years vanishes the more he pursues
wealth. Their different attitudes are explained by their
backgrounds; her family is of the nobility while he is a
mere plebeian bloke. The inconsolable widow Herse
"lives closest to truth" because she remains faithful to
her dead warrior and to the memory of unrepeatable
happiness. Gaiser idealizes Herse Andernoth to the
point of describing her as a Puritan immolated in "her
barbaric splendor" and "terrifying strength"; her need
("Not") is other ("anders") than the materialism she
abhors. Upon an "intellectual" woman who is placed
by Gaiser at a pole opposite to Herse, the novelist
heaps a long invective ending in "Pfui." Soldner, who
reminds Herse of her dead husband, sees himself as a
servitor (Söldner) to life whose mission it is to uncover the "swindle" which the Neu-Spuhlers perpe-
trate. In the course of his diatribes he condemns the
educational system and its "preparation for life" as
nothing more than creating a new generation of ma-
terialists, and he carps at the modernisms of people.
Although he claims that Neu-Spuhlers have learned
nothing from the past, he shows little evidence that he
himself has done so except to admit vaguely that
something had gone wrong. Gaiser crowns Soldner
with martyrdom when he, like Oberstelehn in *Eine
Stimme hebt an,* is virtually ejected from Neu-Spuhl
by authorities who are displeased with his mission. But
it is difficult to sympathize with Soldner; actually he
does not have teaching credentials (perhaps Gaiserian
prophets need none) nor is he able to distinguish
between personal peeves and constructive social criticism.

Having failed to establish satisfying contact with
people and with an environment like Neu-Spuhl,
where does a person such as Soldner find a measure of
contentment? Gaiser conjures up a place, a dream-
scape *Am Pass Nascondo* (1960) where well water

flows "pure and uncontaminated by chlorine," a landscape unspoiled by people, where "one is rid of reptiles." The locale near Nascondo Pass is an exotic composite, with a Mediterranean flavor, of places which attracted Gaiser. Hypnotic and suited to the reverie of the narrator, the prose allows subconscious thoughts and images of persons in one's past to bob to the surface: "Reality was resemblance and resemblance was reality." The interchangeability of the two allows the narrator to relive and wishfully add to his relations with one of the women—Ness—who appeared in *Eine Stimme hebt an*; Herse Andernoth also is revived, but again she eludes him. Nature and death thoughts are closely related and give him a tranquillity and pleasure anticipatory of the time when "beginning and ending" dissolve into one another. When the narrator-writer is faced with the question of whether or not to change any of his previous text, he reflects:

> No additions, no deletions. Yet, I no longer believe in anything. How else? Should I permit myself to be lured again, lured again by things which I do not know and about which I don't want to know? Who would be served by it? Better that I should serve no one.

This gospel of noncommitment, except to a primitive Weltschmerz, may well be the epitaph to Gaiser's writings. Admirers of Gaiser have drawn likenesses between some of Gaiser's characters and Böll's, but these comparisons are misleading. Where Gaiser largely has contempt for people, Böll and other committed writers show compassion and insight, despite satire. Obfuscation rather than enlightenment, evasion rather than critical confrontation with the past, subversion of contemporary society rather than reformation, privatism rather than communality, disciplinary order and power rather than democratic experimentation, all inform Gaiser's fiction. Gaiser's melodies may be seductive—especially for the young who are disillusioned with the world—but the accents are wrong. The twentieth century has suffered enough from blood, soil, Volk, and nature mysticism, as well as from the "instinctual" man. It is tragic that Gaiser has resurrected rather than buried him.

Born in 1934, Uwe Johnson belonged to the generation most pliable to the pressures of the Nazi regime and least knowledgeable about the significance of the events in which it was caught up. Only after the war were the individuals of that generation capable of sizing up their roles—for better or for worse. The relentless search for details reflected in Johnson's novels at the same time allows a composite perspective of the years, roughly, since 1940. Like an ideal reporter, he attempts objectivity and persistently pursues his quarries with questions and more questions. Almost exclusively, Johnson dedicates himself to the phenomenon of the divided Germanies: "the border: the difference: the distance." Although the nature of freedom has been dealt with by philosophers and historians, it gains deeper dimensions in the fiction—or literary journalism—of Johnson.

In the thirties, Johnson grew up in the province of Mecklenburg (southeast of the Jutland peninsula), where he belonged to state youth organizations—both toward the end of the Hitler regime and of the East German regime; then, after high school, he attended the Universities of Rostock and Leipzig, where he studied German language and literature. While a student, he took exception to the official state campaign against the church, although he did not belong to any religious denomination. This independent streak was duly noted on his academic record and he had difficulty finding work after graduation in 1956. Until 1959 he earned a living with the help of friends who provided him with money and writing jobs, including dictionary work, which he could pursue anonymously. He did some translating from the English and could have kept up a silent career in East Germany indefinitely.

After the Khrushchev thaw in 1956, he had the impression that novelists could speak freely; he was disabused of this when he submitted to the authorities a manuscript whose contents were not acceptable. It was a fledgling novel (since discarded) about two Mecklenburg students, in love, who were distressed by the paradox of a state which preached equality for religious creeds but was intent upon suppressing religion. The students decided to go to West Germany. Although the socialist promise of the East was pictured in generally complimentary terms and the West was not, it became quite clear that the book would never see publication in East Germany. Then, two years before the wall was built between East and West Berlin, Johnson passed through West Berlin by train in 1959 and peremptorily got off to stay. That year his novel *Mutmassungen über Jakob* (1959; *Speculations about Jakob*, 1963)—written in the East and published in the West—garnered the Fontane prize of West Berlin and later the International Publishers prize. After that appeared *Das dritte Buch über Achim* (1961; *The Third Book about Achim*, 1967), *Karsch, und andere Prosa,* 1964, and *Zwei Ansichten* (1965; *Two Views,* 1965). His strong interest in modern American literature and American life led him to accept visiting academic posts in 1961 in the United States, taking the opportunity also of touring the country. During 1966 and 1967 he returned for a lecture tour, to attend a sponsored meeting of the "Group 47" at Princeton, and stayed to hold a temporary editorial position in New York City. At an interview he was quoted as saying, "I am destroying beliefs that everyone has tried to establish in me." The battle he has waged to retain objectivity, whether living in the East or the West, is reflected in his novels, which show people in a maze with more blind alleys than open paths.

For Johnson, the materials of one's own experience are all-important to one's writing. As a result, his novels are a painstaking assemblage of knowledge and impressions about the divided German societies. The novelist, though impartial, hopes that the reader will draw valid conclusions from the mass of information presented and the stories told. "Literature," says Johnson in *Speculations about Jakob*, "preserves for us one individual's relationship to the world." However, the deciphering of that relationship and coming to grips with it by the individual or the outside observer are no easy tasks, as we find out in reading the novel. The basic retrospective incidents of the novel are relatively simple but the personal relationships are complex and ambiguous. In a heavy fog during October of 1956 (the time also of the Hungarian uprising) a 28-year-old employee—Jakob Abs—of the East German Railroad "was crossing the tracks on his way to work and had just stepped out of the way of a northbound locomotive . . . when he was scooped up by another locomotive coming from the opposite direction." While the state officially regrets the tragic accident, lauds Jakob's great contribution to the socialist cause, and honors his memory, his friends and associates review the background leading to the event. Through a disarray of third-person narrative, dialogues, monologues, and shifting planes of time and action—which try one's patience inordinately but which at the same time involve one in the laborious quest for truth—certain patterns emerge as well as further doubts.

Jakob had been a man who for seven years worked his way up the ladder to the responsible post of supervising intricate train movement schedules. Of the changes of "seasons he actually noticed only the difference in light." Life was devoted unvaryingly to floating from his job to his furnished room, a routine which not only defined his loyalty and faith in the

state but also made of him a somnambulistic figure—
solid, without characteristics—except for habitual gestures, sad and brusque. When the state coerces him
into accepting a mission to West Germany, it breaks
his routine and with it the dam which has pent up
Jakob's thoughts and delimited his human contacts.
On official and temporary leave, ostensibly to visit his
mother—one of those labeled deserter from the Democratic Republic, Jakob renews an old friendship with
Gesine, who works for (or possibly as an agent
against) NATO headquarters as a translator. She does
not reveal her mission, nor does he. Despite the freedom he encounters in the West, Jakob does not become disloyal to the East. Why? Jakob is put on the
defensive by radio attacks on the East, by the affluence
of the West, by "the smug forgetful faces" of people
who play the Führer's favorite Badenweiler March
("you people are bringing him back to life . . . Nonsense, it's beautiful music"). In sum, to Jakob, the
West is a major evil and the East a minor one; he
really is fooled by no one's slogans. At least, in the
East he is needed as "a part in society." Yet, these are
not the decisive views that alter Jakob; Johnson is no
simplistic reporter. A careful reading of the novel
shows that clues have been strewn throughout showing a progressive corrosion of Jakob's spirit: during his
youth he had watched the dismantling of his country
by occupying forces, had learned about the existence
of concentration camps (a thought "impossible to live
with"); recently he had supervised the Russian military train transports through his area on the way to
crush the Hungarian people's uprising (delay he felt
would have changed nothing); while in the West he
saw proofs of "the inhuman side of capitalism" and
was assailed by fear that free competition might eventually lead to overproduction, mass unemployment,
armaments, war. Distrust of the West, inability to
"bend" or to swallow totally the definition by East
authorities that freedom "is accepting what is neces-

sary" ("That's no help," said Jakob), further dampen Jakob's spirit. Doubts rather than certainties make inroads into his mind; his punctuality and attentiveness slip, he crosses the tracks at a "blind spot," and is crushed trying to avoid juggernaut-like trains coming from the East and the West. A resigned epitaph to Jakob's life and death might be: things just were that way.

One comes away from the novel with the feeling that in the society of the East, people are withdrawn because of mutual suspicions, hoarding their privacy as much as possible, mildly protesting their being "shoved around"; but they are caught helplessly in a web of time and circumstance: "irretrievably lost in time." Robbed of the possibility of assertive action, attention to minutiae and immediate tasks becomes all-consuming. The dependence upon objects to help define one's daily existence was rendered brilliantly in Rainer Maria Rilke's novel *Malte Laurids Brigge* (1910), and has had its impact on modern continental writers and the *roman nouveau*. Objects or things which *are* by virtue of their undeniable existence are isolated and personified through what might be called lyrical pantheism, particularly by such romanciers as Alain Robbe-Grillet. The cue was picked up by Johnson:

> These were tangible durable objects, boxcars, locomotives, coaches; the movement of each completing all others, interdependent, all tied and gathered into a single high-up over-all perspective; every occurrence in Jakob's head corresponded to a reality, something really did happen, shouldn't that make a man feel he was singlehandedly supplying half the day and the area of a small duchy with universal events?

Johnson creates maximum identification—temporary and illusory—between man and object (alien, unemotional, detached) with such calculated and pithy passages as,

A locomotive consists of numerous tons of artfully as-
sembled steel with inhuman strength, it races ahead
wild and irresistible on its tracks and can't escape them
and slams into the switches with all its weight which
grows in proportion to the square of its speed, the heavy
hurry of the power engine is felt in every one of its
parts: . . . after work he [the trainman Jöche] liked to
sit quietly for a while in the house that stood still, at a
window that didn't move, and let the quiver of racing
steel ebb from his nerves at underarms and temples.

Disconcerting, but occasionally lifelike, are the results of Johnson's fusion of thought and its verbaliza-
tion in dialogue and narration. A description of the
technique—with its abrupt and discursive shifts of
tense and perspective—may be found in the novel
itself.

words were not enough too polished threadbare to express the giant maze of proved and assumed facts, tire-
lessly he'd add to his sentences, break them off ruthlessly as soon as they led to something new, he had
completely renounced clocktime and the present, he
moved exclusively in the past that filled his mind with
its time and space.

Johnson's methods have been compared with those of
Joyce and Faulkner, but methods, although they bear
similarities, do not make art. Joyce and Faulkner's
people live through their full and sensual apprehen-
sion of experience; Johnson's people live through their
fragmented and lugubrious cerebrations. One is art
while the other is artifice. Much the same methods
that mark *Speculations about Jakob* also dominate
Johnson's subsequent social novel, *The Third Book
about Achim.*

Again, an ironic and sceptical tone plays over the
actions and speculations that ensue when one attempts to get at truth, but the focus is sharper. A
western journalist visits East Germany in 1960 because of some unexplained and seemingly urgent message from a former girl friend Karin, an actress whose

career fades when she withholds cooperation from the authorities. Although the journalist Karsch seeks no entanglements, he is inveigled into writing still another book about a master bicycle racer named Achim; two that had already been published were not found "usable" by the authorities. Karsch attempts to reconstruct the life of Achim through interviews with many people and by pursuing hints which open up the past. Through inferences, implications, and more indirections than direct observations—memory, after all, is suspiciously subjective—we learn about Achim. During the war years, the youngster had been so thoroughly indoctrinated by the Nazi system that he would have turned his father over to the authorities had he even suspected him of acts of sabotage or of listening to foreign radio broadcasts. Achim belonged to "the coarse-mouthed uniformed youth gang" which roamed the city to capture and beat up escaped prisoners of war. Other entertainment presented itself during the last days of the war:

> . . . at that time he [the young Achim] watched the hanging of a man, he has forgotten what he had been guilty of, smuggling foodstuffs or displaying a white flag, yes, since tanks already cruised through the city, they strung him up, slightly over a man's height the tree had a strong branch onto which one fellow clambered, had to put the sling fairly tight on the branch, another brought a stool from a nearby milk store, and so many people milled around, hardly permitting the soldiers to pass with the puzzled man whose necktie they had torn, from a distance his wife kept screaming quite high unintelligible screams quite far away, he could not get up on the stool by himself, supported by young soldiers looking ready to help, yes, they had ever so honest faces, the necktie he took from his neck on his own wanted to say something beat him with their bare fists not with a rifle stock with fists really looked gentle shoved away the milk stool wellwell he then died quickly he became constantly more elongated after the movement of feet pointed downward and the face turned all colors as he

hung began to twist as they caught him by the pants to
see if he had stiffness and twisted him about again had
obviously no stiffness were however no experts.

Johnson's words revolt against the scene which tran-
scends in horror the capacity of language; a one-para-
graph picture. Someone compares the scene with that
of a theatre whose spectators assume a quiet and pious
attitude. But the comparison is superficial: during the
night some of the quiet and pious ones returned to
strip the body of all its clothing and pick up the teeth
which had fallen to the ground. The narrator's dark
comment is: "Today, all among us live the potential
and the real executioner." The beast is seen lurking
beneath the peaceful and friendly normal everyday
activity and behavior of people. (The contrast between the serenity of nature and the brutal potential
of people also disturbed Jakob and Gesine.) It seems
that the young Achim was deeply affected by the exe-
cution scene and found a pretext to run away from it.
But there were others he could not avoid during the
Allied occupation, especially scenes of Russian frater-
nalism (episodes of violation of humans and collec-
tivizations are etched with brutal and emotionless
precision). Having been sickened temporarily by totalitarianism, Achim somehow becomes involved in the
Berlin workers' uprising of June 1953, and intimations
are that he received a light prison sentence. All this he
must obliterate from his conscious mind during his
swift rise from laborer to folk symbol. Whether in
obligation to the symbolic crown he has achieved or as
a temporizing political convert, Achim defends the
state to all outsiders and deliberately sidetracks his
biographer ("What would you do with the truth?" he
asks Karsch). Of the two requirements that con-
fronted Karsch—that he write a biography extolling
Achim as politically engaged, and that he depict him
as an extraordinary athlete, Karsch can only fulfill the
latter. The racing contests and training are rendered a
bit too minutely but with momentum and expertise.

Achim is not a hero, he is an enigma to himself, friends, and outsiders. Only through fingertip intuition can the reader gain a partial understanding of what makes Achim, Karsch, Karin, and the state officials tick; they resist penetration into heart and mind. To the extent that the author disclaims omniscience, the novel becomes reportage and an ingenious game. Yet the novelty of portraying an honest "attempt at an attempt" to corral truth forces the reader into involvement and participation in the search–a rare accomplishment in the modern novel. With *The Third Book about Achim*, Johnson went beyond the stereotypes so numerous in *Speculations about Jakob*; with *Two Views* he demonstrated a sureness of touch with less unconventional methods.

What he originally started as a documentary book about the West German organization which helped people escape despite the wall that sealed off East Germany in 1961, Johnson turned into a psychological novel. In preparation, he resorted to numerous interviews and gained first-hand experience in the escape operation by bringing over the girl he later married. Rather than jeopardize the security of the escape operation, Johnson gives only a minimum of details about it and concentrates instead on *Two Views*, delineating the issues involved in–as well as the choice between–living under a capitalistic system or a "so-called socialistic organization of society."

Beate (simply represented by the letter D., in the German version, designating East Germany), a young nurse, has grown up in a state which

> described its virtues by the sins of the past state. . . .
> trusting in an open future, and the right to choose the
> other country. Locked in this one, she felt cheated,
> deceived, deluded. . . . an insult one cannot return; it
> squeezed the throat, hindered breathing in a barely
> perceptible way, wanted to be expressed.

The near-total isolation of East Germans is seen through the detailed aggravations endured by Beate.

The other side—and the worst side of western affluence—is represented by Diethbert (B., Bundesrepub-
lik, or West Germany), a footloose, free-lance press
photographer lost in alcoholic sentimentality over the
theft of his luxurious sports car. Through Diethbert,
with whom she has had an affair, Beate manages to
escape to the other Berlin. But she feels no love for
Diethbert—only sympathy; in seriousness of purpose,
she is far beyond him.

In no other novel is the dividedness of the two
Berlins and the two Germanies—culturally and politically—rendered with such precision of language and
feeling. Jakob, Karsch, Karen, Achim, and Beate are
personifications of the anguished internal dialogue
and conflicts taking place. Indeed, an East German
Communist Party newspaper has noted that the differing social developments make it "no longer possible
to speak of one German national language." In the
East German language, Johnson is "Ein Objektivist,"
a person politically unreliable because he sees both
sides of an issue and questions both. Although Johnson knows that "freedom" in the East is obsolete, he
has refused to become a propagandist for the West
either as a novelist or as a public figure. Possibly to
avoid the very tangible pressures that have been placed
upon him, he takes frequent trips abroad. Yet, his
writings speak honestly and clearly of impartial compassion and they report his experiences, without naïve
optimism for the future.

Quite another way of dealing with the raw data of
history and personal experience may be found in the
writings of Günter Grass. His scorn found an exuberant outlet in satire so aggressive and polemical that
only a few German novelists—old and new—can be
called on for comparison. Born in the Free City of
Danzig (presently the Polish city of Gdańsk) in 1927,
Grass has made the seaport and its environs the major

setting for his novels. The son of a German grocer and a mother descended from Kashubians, Slavonic-Pomeranian peasantry, his outlook remained broad despite mandatory service in the Hitler youth movement and as a drafted Luftwaffe aide at the age of sixteen. Wounded in battle and then a prisoner of war, Grass was released in 1946; homeless, he found work in the Rhineland as a farm laborer, worked in a potash mine, became an apprentice to a stonecutter who bartered tombstones on the black market, studied sculpture at the art academy of Düsseldorf, and made extra money as jazz band drummer and washboard accompanist. From 1953 to 1956 he lived in Berlin with his wife, resumed art studies and wrote plays and poetry that came to the attention of "Group 47," which helped him find a publisher and subsidies for his subsequent two-year stay in Paris, where he worked on a novel. Such biographical details—including his political campaigning for the Social Democratic party—are important because they help to explain the incredible diversity of preoccupations and characters in Grass's fiction.

With the publication in 1959 of the novel *Die Blechtrommel* (*The Tin Drum*, 1963), he achieved instant notoriety later sustained by *Katz und Maus* (1961; *Cat and Mouse* 1963), and *Hundejahre* (1963; *Dog Years*, 1965). Together these novels form a panoramic view of modern German history "written in its time," as Grass has said, "looking out of the window and with one's ear turned to the street." Grass's writings have a strong intellectual base. At a Ford Foundation-sponsored literary colloquium held in Berlin in 1964, Grass worked closely with a group of young writers. One of the participants asked him to explore the possibility of a novel based on the life of a man whose vocation it was to shave cadavers. The questioner probably thought that the far-out subject would intrigue Grass. Acknowledging the possibility of coupling many motives in such a novel, Grass however saw no compelling subject matter here but only an exotic idea which, if coolly handled, might make for a secondary figure in a novel but would not provide its substance. Moreover, he felt that a novel requires epic material.

> Take for example the novel *Moby Dick*. It deals only with the fate of an individual, but the total novel is not only coupled to the individual but also is truly permeated with epic material, namely, the whale hunt. Within the epic material there is again a single whale, the white whale which becomes a phantom and then suddenly is real. This I regard as the clamp which holds the novel together. Or take *Berlin Alexanderplatz* by Alfred Döblin. This novel also deals with the fate of an individual. This material without the epic background would constitute the problem of a man released from the Tegel prison and who does not know where to begin. Naturally, this is not sufficient. But when his individual fate is harnessed to the unemployment problem, and is accurately related to the atmosphere of those days, namely the twenties, Döblin has garnered epic material.

As Grass sees it, the epic novel also presupposes knowledge and experience of a kind that made his own and the work of Melville and Döblin possible.

> I speak a bit from experience. In order to earn money, as a sculptor, I lifted death masks and had the opportunity of setting gravestones and to work quite a bit in cemeteries. I know about the commercial aspects of crematoria. That is very dry but also many-faceted material. One would need to give up one's occupation for at least a year and conduct thorough research into the subject: What really happens to dead people? After all, the author of *Moby Dick* spent a good part of his life at sea and dedicated it to the whale hunt.

Grass warns against falling into the temptation of following one's first satiric inspiration; the larger framework is the first necessity. When examining a subject which is capable of sustaining epic material—

like a whale hunt or the federal German army, it is not the author's task to decide if the subject is negative *per se* or to prejudge it, but to accept it as a phenomenon which exists and to test his own opinions through writing about it. Grass follows his own theories.

The epic material of *The Tin Drum* consists mainly of the turbulent years from 1925 to 1955; Grass presupposes that the reader knows the general historical and political outline of the period and the novelist evokes through details a garish atmosphere consistent with the facts of the "phenomenon." At first the picaro, a roguish and black-humored dwarf named Oskar Matzerath, seems a phantom figure out of Grass's luxuriant imagination personifying "the madness of our century," but through insistence he becomes real. At the age of three, Oskar had decided simply not to grow up anymore, refusing to play along with the world of adults; he decided to be anti-social, and to capitalize on the permissiveness extended to children and the feeble-minded. To gain attention he exploited his natural ability to project his screams so fiercely that he shattered glass of every description and at any distance, to the stupid delight of his elders, becoming the subject of a learned article in a medical journal. Oskar not only rejects the world but disturbs its equilibrium by his passion for drums, upon which he sets up fanatic and unendurable noises. He is a master at playing upon peoples' weaknesses. The question of why he is tolerated may well be rephrased to why a potential or actual dictator (who drums evil into skulls) is tolerated.

In his thirtieth year, Oskar finds himself in a mental hospital and from this vantage point leisurely tells his story. Actually there are two Oskars under the same skin: "In those years, I ate decidedly too much cake; as one can ascertain through photographs. Oskar however did not grow taller because of it but stouter and more unshapely." He is the I-narrator and shifts to observe the other "he" as if this part of himself were

detached; he stands at the boundary of the self, looking within and outside. Clearly, Oskar is schizo-
phrenic, alternating between the rational and the mad
in thought and practice, and fluctuates wildly between
the rational and irrational within the breath of one
sentence. What gives Grass's style its fascination and
emotive quality is the fact that many things are going
on simultaneously.

> May our Father in Heaven, the untiring amateur who
> each Sunday snaps us from above, at an unfortunate
> angle that makes for hideous foreshortening, and pastes
> our pictures, properly exposed or not, in His album,
> guide me safely through this album of mine; may He
> deter me from dwelling too long on my favorites and
> discourage Oskar's penchant for the tortuous and laby-
> rinthine; for I am eager to get on from the photographs
> to the originals.

We have here the tone of prayer, the personification
of God to a point of colloquial rather than mystic
familiarity, a spoofing of Grass's own style (its daw-
dling and labyrinthine features), a characterization of
techniques taken from drawing (foreshortened and a
distortion of normal perspective), and an explanation
of narrative intent, namely the interlacing of the factual (photographs, dates, names in the news) and
personal lives. Stalin's death is mentioned in the same
sentence as is the new icebox in Matzerath's delicates-
sen and other miscellaneous items. Max Schmeling's
landing as a paratrooper in Crete, and hurting his
world champion's ankle, is likened to Maria, Oskar's
mother, falling from a ladder. Oskar's relation with
women, who seem to be attracted to the bizarre,
ranges from adoration to the scatological because, as
he explains it, Oskar veers from a Goethe to a Raspu-
tin complex—one is the "luminous poet prince" who
let himself be captivated by women, while the other is
"the dark spirit who cast a spell upon women." Böll
and Johnson, too, were critical of the holy fervor of

"the breathless assembly of childbearers" (Johnson) who dedicated themselves to the Third Reich.

Consistent with Oskar's childlike "innocence," he can see the emperor without clothes. Grass prefers the starkly visual to the editorial approach. We learn through seeing, and by experiencing through negative emotionality, as when a heap of synagogue furnishings "were put to the torch and the grocer [Oskar's father] used the opportunity to warm his fingers and his feelings over the public bonfire." Felt in many of the episodes that further Oskar's education is a hushed horror. Perceptively, the critic Marcel Reich-Ranicki has noted, "Grass avoids the sentimentalizing of Jews, making Poles heroic, and the demonizing of Nazis; National Socialism does not interest him as a political movement or as a sociological phenomenon," rather he is interested in its effects on people and their behavior. In many German postwar novels, we find considerable sympathy extended by the authors to minorities and victims, giving readers a self-satisfied glow. In Grass, however, sympathy and sentimentality seem absent, as in the following capsule-scene:

> I [Oskar] found them [the Nazis] still at play when I, also through the window, entered the shop. Some had taken their pants down and had deposited brown sausages, in which half-digested peas were still discernible, on sailing vessels, fiddling monkeys, and on my drums. . . . One had drawn his dagger. He was cutting dolls open and he seemed disappointed each time that nothing but sawdust flowed from their limbs and bodies.

> The toy merchant sat behind his desk. As usual he had on sleeve protectors over his dark-grey everyday jacket. Dandruff on his shoulders showed that his scalp was in bad shape. One of the SA men with puppets on his fingers poked him with Kasperl's wooden grandmother, but Markus was beyond being spoken to, beyond being hurt or humiliated. Before him on the desk stood an empty water glass; the sound of his crashing shop-window had made him thirsty no doubt.

This scene contains neither opprobrious adjectives for the villains nor sympathetic ones for the victim. The actions speak for themselves: persecutors appear like mindless animals, while the unheroic victim looks like a forlorn scrap of humanity. Grass's art is an act of provocation: he stings the reader to laughter, anger, embarrassment, and reflection. Particularly effective are short incisive scenes: patriots defending the Polish post office in Danzig in December 1939 against the Germans; the Markus incident which reflects one of thousands during the infamous Crystal Night of 1938; and the unnerving scene in a cellar where several families had taken refuge only to be discovered by a group of Russian soldiers. There Oskar's father, who had "warmed his feelings on the bonfire" mentioned, swallows his Nazi party pin and chokes to death; literally and figuratively the party is over.

The grotesque and real are so skilfully blended that one has to look to Grass's mentors—Rabelais, Laurence Sterne, Dos Passos, Joyce—or to parts of John Barth's writing and to the military preinduction scene of Thomas Mann's *Felix Krull* to find parallel artistic triumphs. Probably Grass's best example of surrealistic and thematic fantasy relates to Schmuh's *Onion Cellar*, a supposedly West German subterranean night club, lighted by acetylene lamps and furnished with onion-sack covered crates on which customers sat uncomfortably; it was a night club without menus or a bar. The clientele consisted of a complete cross-section of the intellectual world and people came to talk, to unburden themselves. It was a vast house of penance. Yet, despite their eagerness, they could not get started until they began to peel onions with paring knives.

> Onions—onions such as were represented, golden-yellow and slightly stylized . . . plain, ordinary onions, not tulip bulbs, but onions such as women buy in the market place, such as a vegetable woman sells, such as the peasant, the peasant's wife, or the hired girl plants and harvests, onions such as may be seen more or less

faithfully portrayed in the still life of the lesser Dutch masters.

What was the result: Tears of deliverance and release were shed.

> . . . they could see nothing more, because their eyes were running over, and not because their hearts were so full; for it is not true when the heart is full the eyes necessarily overflow, some people can never manage it, especially in our century, which in spite of all the suffering and sorrow will surely be known to posterity as the tearless century. It was this drought, this tearlessness, that brought those who could afford it to Schmuh's onion cellar . . . what did the onion juice do? It did what the world and the sorrows of the world could not do: it brought forth a round, human tear. It made them cry. At last they were able to cry again. To cry properly, without restraint, to cry like mad. The tears flowed and washed everything away. The rains came.

The moral is clear and reminds one of the declared need of Borchert's characters to become human again. While Borchert is desperately optimistic that this can be so, Grass points to the artificiality of such self-induced sentiment. Adults can find fulfillment the week around while students can take advantage of onions at half price on Mondays. Grass ingeniously exploits the drama in the onion cellar and improvises comic subthemes. For instance, when the customers at one time indulge in two onions instead of the customary one, only a mild orgy—according to the disappointed Oskar—takes place, and the musicians, sparked by Oskar's drumming, take up their instruments and restore "normalcy." But Oskar's career in the onion cellar during 1950 was short-lived, for the owner was unwilling to forgive him for a drum solo that had transformed his well-paying guests into "babbling, riotously merry children who wet their pants and cried because they had wet their pants, all without the benefit of onions." Suggestive, indeed, is the fact that the maniacal drummer had been able to reduce even an intellectual audience to infantilism.

No one in the *petit-bourgeois* world comes off well; all feel the lash of Grass's satire: officialdom, religious institutions, the professions. Grass has not disguised his conviction that the German recovery came too early, brought too much wealth, too little soul searching, and no exorcism of the past. Oskar's ascent and descent are not final; he serenely bides his time in a mental institution and his drum is not out of reach.

Grass's second novel, *Cat and Mouse*, is comparatively subdued and short. Oskar appears several times in the background—once as a mascot to a gang of church desecrators—and new characters are introduced which we hear from again in *Dog Years*. In the center of things is Joachim Mahlke, disfigured by a monstrous Adam's apple (the "mouse") which he tries to hide with a multitude of decorative items from a screw driver to religious medallions. Though admired by a group of juveniles for his gymnastic prowess, his diving and retrieving of objects from a sunken boat, and as winner of a maleness contest, the "Great Mahlke" still feels an apartness from the normal "cats" whose pranks emphasize his freakishness, causing emotional hurt and turning his young thoughts toward becoming a clown. His lonely quest for certainty and solace turn into "excessive religious fervor" directed toward the protective figure of the Virgin Mary, bringing him close to the "border of pagan idolatry" rather than spiritual worship. At the same time he is torn between the need to prove himself as an individual by the standards of his society, and his contempt for those standards. Visiting Mahlke's school—and Grass's portrayals of Danzig school life under the Nazis are particularly incisive, a U-boat commander gives a pep talk and ostentatiously displays a knight's cross earned in combat. Mahlke ingeniously steals the cross and gives it a place of honor over his private parts. The theft causes a furor, Mahlke joins the army and earns his own medal, overstays a home furlough and drowns while trying to duplicate earlier diving feats. Possibly it was suicide, for Mahlke had his fill of the world as it was. In a style that shows considerable finesse and control of the colloquial, the novel quietly tells of the quixotic attempts of an individual to rebel against unthinking conformity, and his defeat.

What could more logically follow cat and mouse, if not dog? The title *Dog Years* gives notice that Grass strongly literalizes the colloquial and exposes what was common, in the pejorative sense. Specifically, during the years of the Third Reich, Germany went to the dogs, while the postwar years constituted the tail end. It was as if the enormousness and enormities of events past and present had to wait for dimensional retelling by a novelist with Grass's arsenal. In 1575 Johann Fischart, castigating his own times, launched a free-wheeling German adaptation of Rabelais' *Gargantua* (*Affenteurliche und ungeheurliche Geschichtschrift vom Leben, Rhaten und Thaten . . .*). Not until Grass do we find a German novelist with the same insatiable appetite for words and a linguistic power directed toward cajoling, exacerbating, scandalizing, and angering as well as delighting readers. Everything in Grass's *Dog Years* has baroque motion and brute force. Descriptions and monologues are torrential; every style from the bureaucratic to the philosophical is parodied; indignation boils over in a lava of disrespectful adjectives; Oskarian grossnesses dominate; encyclopedic accounts of local sports and history and outrageous inventiveness proliferate. Yet, everything is grounded in fact. Isolated novels like Fischart's or Grimmelshausen's (*Simplicissimus*, 1669) do not make a tradition; on the contrary, like them *Dog Years* is out of the mainstream, defying the passion for "order" and tidied structuredness of German literature even in the so-called modern experimental novel.

Three narrators comb over the past and relate it to the present, giving the novel a chaotic appearance because of the winding stream of episodes and evident repetitions; yet the repetitions also embody different perspectives. What gives the novel unity are the insistent historical chronology, its convergent lines of narrative development, its essential fable, and thematic variations of basic notations. In discussing the novel one is tempted to escalate the literal into the metaphorical as Grass does. Literally, as a token of esteem the people in the Danzig area give the Führer a shepherd dog called Prince; metaphorically, during the end of the Third Reich the dog is returned by the Führer to the people, their legacy. As the radio plays Wagner's "Götterdämmerung," a communiqué is read: "Führer passed away yesterday one five three 0 hours. Testament in force and on way. As per instructions April 29, Führer's favorite dog Prinz, black, short-haired, shepherd, is Führer's gift to the German people. Acknowledge receipt." But, through the Concordat the Vatican too is legatee of the "dog": "Dog Prinz will try to reach Vatican City. If Pacelli raises claims, protest immediately and invoke codicil to will." Grass exploits every nuance of a given idea.

The dog is demonized and "humanized." It is a black and vicious historical force; it is called a Nazi, and people exhibit their inclinations by their association with the dog. Tulla Pokriefke, a scabrous girl—an instigator of evil, lies down with the dog in its shed; the ex-Nazi Walter Matern cannot shake the dog which attaches itself to him in his postwar Odyssey through West and East Germany; Herr Liebenau—the dog breeder—destroys the dog shed after realizing the consequences of Nazism, and Hitler places the dog on the same level as his personal cohorts. With the same zeal that characterized the Nazis' investigation of people's genealogy to determine pure Aryanism, the dog's background is searched and found pure—he even has mythological ancestors. Grass makes it clear that the "dog" is a German phenomenon, purebred, a hound of hell.

On another level, *Dog Years* is a version of the Cain and Abel story ("What brotherly joy round Cain and

Abel, for who God journeyed through the clouds—
causa-genetic, Haïssable [hateful]: the late I"—
quoted by Grass from a Benn poem). A deep-rooted
psychological relationship of hate and love and sadism
and masochism develops between the storm trooper
Walter Matern and the half-Jew Eduard Amsel.
Growing up together, Walter protects Eddi against
the "kike"-taunting bullies and they seal a blood-
brothership, but he throws away a jacknife which Eddi
offered in friendship. Nevertheless, Walter becomes a
business partner to the artistic Eddi, who creates
sought-after lifelike scarecrows. Later Walter joins the
Communist Party but shifts over to the Nazis who
promise more beer and excitement. To prove himself
on the right side, Walter leads a crew of eight troopers
who beat Eddi into a bloody pulp. Eddi vanishes,
assumes different names and variously survives as a
ballet director, publisher, and salt mine owner. After
the war, Walter compulsively seeks out Eddi, is offered the boyhood knife which Eddi has found, but
rejects it again.

Grass's honesty is above question. He writes within
the limits of what he knows and determinedly probes
into areas he likes to know more about—with mixed
results. One such area is the psychological twinship of
Walter and Eddi. Walter's type of latent and aggressive sadism, punctuated by periods of guilt feelings,
takes the irrational but opportunistic form of pursuing
a victim when society encourages him to do so and
then claiming the friendship of the victim when the
climate has changed. What about Eddi? And here
Grass seems to say that a man becomes the stereotype
which society's prejudices force him to be. Beyond
that there is the dark speculation that the victim has a
predisposition to become a masochistic stereotype.
Eddi's father assiduously studied and annotated the
peculiar work *Geschlecht und Charakter* (1903; *Sex
and Character*) by Otto Weininger; Eddi inherited
the book, declaimed from it, and was poisoned by the
"devil's work."

At the turn of the century Austrian cultural life received its ferment from a group of men of Jewish descent in the arts and sciences—like Schnitzler and Freud—and on its fringes was Weininger, misshapen in body but brilliant of mind, who committed suicide young because he was devoured by a *moi haïsable,* a self-hatred that stemmed from inferiority feelings related to his origins and frustrated sexuality (which he called the negation of ethics) occasioned by inability to establish normal relationships with men or women. Ingenuity and madness merged in Weininger as he went a step beyond the popular biological and metaphysical race theories of Wagner and Houston Stewart Chamberlain; he postulated that women and Jews find contentment in being oppressed, are incapable of genius, possess no soul, no identity or "I." Further, he adopted all anti-Semitic epithets current and combined them to define "Jewishness": arrogance, aggressiveness, mobility, destructive and satiric inclinations, and the like. However, said Weininger, aggressive Anti-Semites like Richard Wagner also possess "Jewishness" and consequently hate these "characteristics" in others. The blood brother relationship between Grass's Walter and Eddi is played out precisely along the lines laid down by Weininger's fantasy. (No thought is given in the novel to the appeal to "legalized looting," economic, and cultural envy—half of Germany's Nobel prize winners were Jewish—as factors in the thirties.) The popular predisposition to accept the unreality of Weininger's six-hundred-page book as factual was evident in the publication by 1927 of twenty-six editions. No wonder then that Walter's father took a cue from Weininger and like him became a convert in order to conquer within himself the characteristics which he thought ruined his existence. To acquire opposite characteristics, father and son threw themselves into "Aryan" sports and church singing; yet, no matter what Eddi does, the shadow of Walter looms large over him.

Grass objects to critics who find symbolism he never

intended in his works. He may be right in the sense that symbolists infer "eternal truths" from petty events and persons, while he himself strives for the truth of a given moment in time and in the specific behavior of individuals in a specific place. Intended or not, Grass's "tin drum" or "dog" are symbolic in addition to their very literal existence. More important, however, are the multitudinous associations deliberately developed and linked by thematic repetition and variation. As in Joyce's *Ulysses*, we find in *Dog Years* that a Homeric kind of narrative—suspenseful and conclusive—is rejected in favor of factual and fictional coincidences stretching through the novel. When Weininger's book appeared in 1903, he was 23-years-old, had premonitory nightmares about a barking dog, and committed suicide several months later. In Grass's *Dog Years* the number 23 and its reversed form, 32, became important: 32 dates the Third Reich; 32 is the number of human teeth which Eddi replaced with gold teeth after Walter's ferocious assault which knocked the joy of life out of Eddi; 32 Nazi saloon-battles take place; the good old days are represented by a 32-volume conversation lexicon still in use during the postwar days; it took 23 years (1932–55) before "magic glasses" were manufactured for the young generation squarely to see the bestial work of their elders; at a forum, 32 youngsters with 32 questions open up the past and indict Walter who collapses (but his ability to forget allows him—as it allows others—to recuperate); Eddi conducts Walter on a tour of his mine—a Dantesque inferno—which has 32 stalls, with focus on stall 23, scornfully called "inner emigration" —a hiding place for acrobats ("It's warm inside . . . there's nobody to bother you").

Aside from numerological coincidences, other thematic linkages give the novel an internal tightness. Walter Matern(a) is descended from notorious medieval firesetters and also is called a "grinder," known for his ferocious gnashing of teeth. He pursues Eddi

Amsel (meaning blackbird) who changes his name to Hase[rabbit]loff. Sawatzki, no matter how denazified, still represents the swastika. Grass packs outrage into brief phraseology (the effluvia from a crematorium chimney becomes "Protestant smog"); he demands a language without subterfuge and mercilessly parodies the obscurities of Heidegger ("Jutting out into the Nothing, the dog has surpassed the essential and will as now be referred to as Transcendence"). Grass is a master of parody and possesses the most remarkable linguistic virtuosity of present German novelists.

If Eddi reviews the past with nausea and anticipates the future with wry scepticism, who can blame him?

> Ah, how mysterious the Germans are, how full of the forgetfulness which is pleasing to God! Not giving it another thought, they cook their pea soup on blue gas flames. . . . what other country in the world can boast such brown, velvety gravies?

> . . . Of course you may say that every man is a potential scarecrow; for after all, this should never be forgotten, the scarecrow was created in man's image. All nations are arsenals of scarecrows. But among them all, it is the Germans, first and foremost, even more so than the Jews, who have it in them to give the world the archetypal scarecrow someday.

Grass modifies the Weininger formula but removes from no one the potential for mechanical and thoughtless behavior.

Should there be a sequel to the adventures of Amsel, it will probably be influenced by Grass's reaction to the Arab-Israeli conflict of 1967. In a newspaper interview, Grass said that Germans "experienced a sincere upsurge of sympathy for the bravery of the Jews in their struggle to protect their homeland and have a dignified life." Grass also noted that, "Up to now, much of the dialogue about the fate of the Jews in Germany was haunted by conscious or unconscious guilt or impeded by recrimination." By extension one might say that the past also has hindered such feelings by Germans for other minorities and nations victimized by the Third Reich. Perhaps the dam is being broken.

Essentially, *Dog Years*, reflects the complexity of human relations, the "organized madness"—as Grass notes—of the years during the Third Reich, the menace of nationalism, and the menace of callousness and indifference among humans. In the last line Grass points by analogy to the root of the matter: "We're . . . naked. Each of us bathes by himself."

Political events, ideologies, and social observations are the dyes which strongly color the German postwar novel. Aside from the novelists discussed, who have gained international reputations, there are others also vitally concerned with literature and language as "the shield of freedom," as Böll put it. Their number and accomplishments are substantial: Alfred Andersch, Christian Geissler, Herman Kasack, Wolfgang Koeppen, Siegfried Lenz, Heinz Erich Nossack, Wolfdietrich Schnurre, Martin Walser. By asking irreverent questions and expressing general dissent, they have caused for themselves no easy time. But except for Wilfred Schilling (*Der Angstmacher*, 1960; *The Fearmakers*, 1959) who fled to Belgium, and a few novelists who were pressured into toning things down, they have stood their ground against furor. Grass, and others, have scored West German society for its materialism, its militarism, and its governing structure that is "soaked through with old Nazis;" yet their distaste for East German totalitarianism is even greater. Their own form of pressure upon society, however, is valuable, constituting the most persuasive educational force to enlighten the West Germans who were born after Hitler's rise—and these constitute half of the total fifty-three million. Many of the older generation want to forget, while all of the younger need to know and some want to know. The principle to which the novelists seem to subscribe is Santayana's phrase: "Those who cannot remember the past are condemned to repeat it." Much of the "documentary" aspect of German plays and novels is rooted in such a tangible fear. It explains, for example, Grass' dedication—as well as that of others in "Group 47"—to "practical politics rather than theoretical ideologies" and warning the young people to shun the fakeries of the growing, recrudescent Nazi party.

Although dissenters like some of the novelists discussed, of necessity, present their views in negative shades, there is promise that their perspectives and sympathies will become enlarged. Contacts with other people, places, and writers through travel and symposia, and two-way translation of fiction and non-fiction are creating a wider cosmopolitan outlook than before. The proof will lie in future novels that reflect the expanded consciousness of both writer and audience. All this may be a far way off because the seeds of disillusionment are too widespread, the danger of again seeking scapegoats if the economy hits rough pockets is everpresent, and the constant irritation and problematic aspects of the two Germanies—their conflicting alliances—and the Berlin wall keep emotions high. The new generation has inherited unenviable legacies. How these are dealt with, the new novelists will let us know.

The Italian Novel
Traditions and New Paths

LOUIS TENENBAUM

The novelist Italo Calvino expressed directly and simply the feeling of many people concerned with contemporary Italian fiction when he stated in 1960: "I
believe that Italian literature is one of the richest and
most alive today, but the more I believe it, the harder
it is for me to describe it. It is like describing the
Phoenix." [1] Students of recent Italian literature must
share, too, Calvino's envy of a French writer who was,
like himself in 1960, visiting the United States on a
Ford Foundation grant and who could, as Calvino
could not, speak with precision about what contemporary French writers are up to, mainly because of the
orderly habit of the French in defining to themselves
and to the world just what they are trying to do and
then giving it a neat label. It is no easier since then to
attempt with any reasonable hope of success, the task
which had discouraged Calvino in 1960, because the
vitality and variety of fiction published in Italy has
continued unabated and few main currents or groupings of narrators have emerged for critical or historical
appraisal. Italian writers have had a disconcerting
tendency to escape from or to avoid labels, even in
periods when they are most strongly tempted to follow
some literary leader or some cultural or esthetic trend.
Perhaps the most potent example of the independence
of the Italian literary man is the inability of the
twenty-year Fascist dictatorship to produce a "Fascist"
literature.

Another pertinent factor accounting for the individualism of the Italian novelist is that Italians came to the field of long narrative fiction comparatively late. Literary historians repeatedly point to the lack of a real tradition of the novel in Italy and it is by now a cliché to speak of the dominant role of poetry and the pre-eminence of *prosa d'arte* in her literary culture. The Italian novel was born when Alessandro Manzoni wrote *I promessi sposi* (*The Betrothed*), the richly textured historical novel of life under Spanish despotism in seventeenth-century Lombardy, whose first version belongs to the years 1821–23 but whose definitive edition dates from about 1840. In spite of the enormous artistic, linguistic, and historical importance of *I promessi sposi* (numerous Italian writers of the twentieth century acknowledge the direct or indirect influence of Manzoni on their own artistic formation), the writer with the most powerful appeal to the contemporary temper has been the Catanian Giovanni Verga whose masterpieces, *I Malavoglia* (translated first by D. H. Lawrence as *The House by the Medlar Tree*) and *Mastro-don Gesualdo* were published respectively in 1881 and 1888. Unjustly neglected for almost thirty years, Verga's novels and shorter fiction came to have a vital, inspiriting influence on the work of the following two literary generations. These are the two generations which speak most effectively to our time.

The word "contemporary" applies to the narrative fiction published in Italy from approximately 1930 to the present, a period encompassing the work of "the second generation," the group which came to maturity during the last decade of the Fascist period and is continuing after the debacle of World War II to provide Italy's most authoritative voice in literature. Since the end of the war we have begun to hear the increasingly convincing and powerful voice of "the third generation," in many ways linked to its predecessor, which has begun to take on its own special coloration and character. The most important nonliterary influences brought to bear on the moral, social, political, and philosophical formation of these two generations have been obviously the Fascist dictatorship and the war. The totality of both these experiences could leave no sensitive writer untouched, and even today some of the most significant works being published continue to reflect that past.

Contemporary Italian fiction has often tried to mirror the spiritual and moral condition of Italy between two world wars, particularly the sterility and intellectual despair of the last ten years of Fascism. It includes a literature about war, produced by participants in the military campaigns outside of Italy. Part of this war literature, but distinct from it, is the literature of the Resistance, the bitter civil-war which helped re-establish the self-respect of the Italian people. Most importantly, today's Italian writers have felt the need to search, among the physical and spiritual ruins of postwar Italy, for essential definitions and meanings, for ideals and values which had been corrupted and obscured by Fascism, by the horrors of the military struggle, by the blind and conflicting political forces which have come out of the war period. Much of contemporary Italian fiction then is a literature of participation, and the representative novelists of the two literary generations which most concern us here, like the French writer Albert Camus, are primarily interested in man's dignity, his relationship to his fellow man, and his search for essential values and meaning in a world which has abandoned traditional sources of guidance. The concern of the contemporary novelist in Italy often centers on an essential dualism: man's sense of responsibility to himself as an individual, and his need for a bond of companionship, of love toward his fellows in a close and meaningful social relationship.

While Italian literature was harassed and sometimes hamstrung by Fascist censorship, the really serious difficulties it faced were more indirect and bound to the sterility of the spiritual, moral, and political atmosphere. The regime's attempt to nationalize culture and encourage the creation of an official literature was a ridiculous failure; and the Fascists were inclined to leave undisturbed those men of letters who did not openly attempt to stir up trouble in their writings. Thus, there were no obstacles in the early years of their publication to impede the growing influence of two literary reviews in Florence, *Solaria* (founded in 1926) and *Letteratura* (founded as *Solaria*'s successor in 1937) which encouraged and published work by the novelists and poets of the second generation. These magazines were created as part of an attempt to synthesize the precepts of two divergent groups then exerting considerable influence upon literature: the *Rondisti* (attached to the Roman literary and cultural review *La Ronda*), who propounded the all-importance of form and style, and the *Novecentisti* (loyal to the Florentine periodical *Il Novecento*), who supported the need for new, more European content in Italian writing. Out of the ferment of this new movement, headquartered in Florence, have come the names and works of some of the outstanding writers of the contemporary period: Alberto Moravia, Cesare Pavese, Elio Vittorini, Carlo Emilio Gadda, Gianna Manzini, among others. The *Solaria-Letteratura* "axis" can be credited with focusing attention on the works of the important Triestino writer, Italo Svevo, friend, disciple, and perhaps influence on James Joyce. Until brought to public notice by the Solariano poet Eugenio Montale, Svevo was relatively unknown in Italy. It was in this atmosphere that the contributions of Stendhal, Proust, Joyce, Kafka, and Gide to European literature and culture were discussed and the lessons assimilated. The late Elio Vittorini, a leading spokesman for the second generation, paid tribute to both literary reviews, but with an especial warmth of feeling for *Solaria* (where his first stories were published) in a statement undoubtedly echoing the sentiments of his fellow contributors and collaborators. He wrote (in his *Diario in pubblico*, published in 1957): "Thus I was a Solariano, and Solariano was a word which in the literary circles of those days meant anti-Fascist, European, universalist, anti-traditionalist . . . We were insulted on one side by Giovanni Papini and by Farinacci [2] on the other. They also called us dirty Jews because of the hospitality we extended to Jewish writers and because of the good things we had to say about Kafka and Joyce . . ." [3]

The preoccupation of the Solariani and the writers published in *Letteratura* with Europeanizing and universalizing Italian literature in the late twenties and in the thirties is more understandable if we take into account the importance of regionalism in the Italian narrative literature of the first quarter of the century. It was, paradoxically, Giovanni Verga who had supplied the greatest impetus to that literary emphasis whose triumph was symbolized by the award of a Nobel prize in 1936 to the Sardinian novelist Grazia Deledda. What the Solariani and the Europeanizers sought was not so much an elimination of regionalism, as an infusion of broader themes in the work of Italian writers, who more than most Europeans are predestined to a concern with their region because of the facts of Italian geography and history. In this respect the Europeanizers have had a salutary influence on the development of the contemporary novel, with the successful blending of regionalism and universality to be seen in the writings of Cesare Pavese, Vittorini, Ignazio Silone, Carlo Levi, Vasco Pratolini, Vitaliano Brancati, Corrado Alvaro, Giorgio Bassani, and other successful novelists of the second generation.

In their concern with broadening the vision of and infusing new life into Italian narrative literature, the two most important Solariani went across the Atlantic to America for inspiration. Pavese and Vittorini are chiefly responsible for the vogue of American literature which came as an invigorating transfusion into the Italian fiction of the thirties and forties, providing a stimulant lasting until the early postwar period.[4] Calvino, one of the leading novelists of the third generation and a disciple of both Pavese and Vittorini, has succinctly described the literary climate they created by means of their translations of and essays on such writers as Melville, Hawthorne, Whitman, Mark Twain, Sherwood Anderson, and others:

> For Pavese, America was a country which had built a literature bound to the doings of men, the hunting of whales, the planting of cornfields, the building of industrial cities; thus creating new myths that had the force of primordial symbols of consciousness, and creating a new poetic language from the vernacular.
>
> For Vittorini, American literature was an enormous reserve of natural vitality, an ideal battlefield for the contest between new stylistic inventions and academic traditions, between passions of weariness and fury and the weight of inveterate hypocrisies and morals.
>
> For both of them American literature, which is so far from our tradition, let us approach that tradition in a new spirit; and it was with different eyes that we re-read Giovanni Verga . . . with his miraculous modernity of language.
>
> Political reasons—in those last years of Fascism— were mixed with literary ones. America was a gigantic allegory of our Italian problems at that time, of our good qualities and our bad, of our conservatism and our need for rebellion, of our South and our North, of our mosaic of peoples and dialects, of Pavese's Piedmont and Vittorini's Sicily; it was a theatre where we saw rehearsed in an explicit and extreme manner dramas not dissimilar to our own, those hidden dramas of which we were forbidden to speak.[5]

Solaria and *Letteratura*, then, are names suggestive of the renewed approach by Italian writers to the problems of literary expression in fiction, an approach which brought Europe, America, and the neglected writers of Italy's own recent past together to enliven contemporary Italian writing.

The initial flowering of the new Italian literature was the movement which comes closest to having the characteristics of a school of writing, neorealism. The first expression of modern Italian literature to seize the attention and imagination of a sizeable American readership, neorealism was the child of two fathers, Pavese and Vittorini, who transmitted to it their passionate concern with the American writers of the 1930's. The matrix of this new writing was to be an Italy emerging from the spiritual, moral, and physical chaos of the war years. Lacking a true leader and a precisely defined doctrine, the phenomenon can more accurately be called a literary current or a state of mind rather than a school, although Carlo Levi's narrative essay-diary *Cristo si è fermato a Eboli* (1945; *Christ Stopped at Eboli*, 1947) had set a tone, at least from the viewpoint of content and spirit, for a good deal of the fiction which was to be called neorealistic.

Levi revealed the existence in Southern Italy of a segment of society doomed to almost hopeless misery and privation because of a lack of social and governmental concern. This discovery by an enlightened Northerner of the cancer of southern feudalism in a region where men were less than Christians parallels and reaffirms a discovery made by Elio Vittorini, reflected in his *Conversazione in Sicilia* published in 1941 (translated in 1948 as *In Sicily*); it was almost immediately censored by the Fascist regime. Both works underline important tendencies of neorealism, tendencies encouraged and strengthened by the political and social optimism which swept over Italy with the downfall of the twenty-year Fascist dictatorship and the end of the war: a courageous search for truth, an intense concern with a suffering and dolorous humanity, a renewed interest in the life and conditions of the social classes excluded from literature since the end of the nineteenth century, and a somewhat vague neo-Marxist ideological bias which reflected a sense of commitment on the writer's part but which rarely degenerated into political polemic. These qualities of neorealistic writing were shared with the cinema of the time in film classics produced by directors and scenarists like Roberto Rossellini, Vittorio de Sica, Cesare Zavattini, and others.

A new interest in an objective and factual reality was common to both fiction and cinema and was reflected in the vogue for the documentary approach to art. We may see this in part as an extreme reaction —at least in fiction—against indulgent autobiographism and beautifully turned lyric fragments characteristic of prewar prose narrative in Italy. In the emphatic sweeping away of prewar literature which was oblivious to moral and social problems, the neorealists concentrated on the relationship of the individual to his society, investigating the interaction between the private and the social-political. Traditional literary qualities of purism and ornateness, flowery and rhetorical language were rejected by the neorealists who demonstrated a new preference for simplicity, brevity, concreteness, understatement, and a mimetic function for language much in the manner of the American social realist novelists of the 1930's. The rich outpouring of fiction from writers in the immediate postwar period stressed varying aspects of the neorealistic mood, but in the final analysis few works of enduring value remained. Social, economic, and political realities required a sense of perspective which one could hardly expect from the many "liberated" writers who were reveling in their new relationship to truth, to objects, things, and the facts of the new Italy. In the resulting crudity and taste for action and violence, in the direct, linear relationship between the author and observed reality, and the exclusion of reflection, analysis, and especially atmosphere we can see the influence of the Americans. Pavese was reacting to this when he commented somewhat bitterly in 1950 that the American writers had no more to teach the Italians. Pavese himself and Vittorini had made better use in their fiction of American examples; this was possible because their encounter with American writing came as an enrichment to literary sensibilities capable of profiting by that experience.

As the fervor of the earlier postwar years diminished, a closer examination of the neorealistic formula as an instrument for viable criticism brought serious questioning by people like Vittorini. Neorealism as a term encompassed too much in grouping together the diverse approaches to fiction by Alberto Moravia, Pavese, Ignazio Silone, Carlo Levi, Guiseppe Berto, Vitaliano Brancati, Dino Buzzati, and Vasco Pratolini. Vittorini was not satisfied with Sergio Solmi's definition of neorealism as "a certain movement of the chronicle into literature and in parallel fashion an attention brought to bear on certain aspects of the crudest reality, more bound to the material and physiological conditions of life . . ." [6] Vittorini thought that this emphasis had already characterized nineteenth-century verismo (the Italian version of French naturalism). Perhaps he complicated the matter even further when he described as neorealistic the works of fiction he had written in the 1930's, the short stories of *Piccola borghesia* (1931), and the novel *Il garofano rosso* (1948, in book form; *The Red Carnation*, 1952), as well as *Conversazione in Sicilia* which he composed in 1939. Vittorini saw validity in either of two ways for the novelist to attain truth: realism or neorealism. To him realism means the presentation of a new aspect of reality in a new formal structure, whereas neorealism is a reworking of aspects of reality already known and acquired by literature. [7] This broader outlook makes necessary a whole new critical attitude toward the fiction of the postwar period, and puts into serious doubt the validity of the term neorealism as it had been previously used and understood. In essence, he shifted the emphasis from content and ideology to one on literary language and technique. Yet one thing is certain: the shift has raised more critical problems than it has solved. It is possible, for example, to speak of a neorealist Pavese, a neorealist Vittorini, a neorealist Moravia on the basis of certain works, but also to argue that they do not belong in the current on the basis of other works. The critical confusion is reflected in observations by some that Pavese is too personal, too lyrical, too full of existential anguish, and too concerned with myth to be a consistent neorealist. The sociological aspect of neorealism is satisfied by Vittorini's fiction, but a restrictive interpretation must find the symbolism-laden tensions of his essentially poetic and lyrically conceived narrative world hard to include in a neorealist category. Moravia's preoccupation with psychological analysis and the existential alienation depicted in so much of his work also make it difficult to consider him exclusively as a neorealist.

One of the most successful illustrations of Vittorini's interpretation of neorealism in postwar fiction can be found in the work of Vasco Pratolini, although it is significant to note that the essential themes and motifs of his narrative predate the war. Pratolini is the novelist par excellence of Florentine working class life and society and his *Il Quartiere* (1945; *The Naked Streets*, 1952) and *Cronache di poveri amanti* (1947; *A Tale of Poor Lovers*, 1949) are considered classics of the neorealistic mood and manner. He was extremely successful in combining in these works a realistic description of the everyday life of the Florentine proletariat, with an elegiac atmosphere, reflecting a deep spiritual involvement on his own part. The idealistic concern with human and social solidarity so characteristic of the early postwar years is admirably expressed by Pratolini in these works. While they can exemplify the success of neorealism as a novelistic current, Pratolini's succeeding work has ironically come to stand for the "crisis of neorealism" which has crystallized around the publication of a novel, *Metello*, in 1955. This is the first book of a trilogy published with the general title *Una storia italiana*. Pratolini's artistic intent was to enrich neorealism which he saw as badly needing a sense of historical perspective. History came to replace chronicle in this series of novels depicting nearly one hundred years of social, economic, and moral life in Italy. *Metello* put the focus first on the development of an organized working class in the newly unified nation and it tells the story of a Socialist bricklayer set against a background of political and economic struggle. *Lo scialo* (1960; *The Waste*) covers the years 1910 to 1930 in an examination of the lives of the bourgeoisie seen from within and with a group emphasis, rather than an individual one. In this long novel Pratolini was able to focus on the phenomenon of Fascism as a destructive influence on a number of middle-class families. *Allegoria e derisione* (1966) completes the trilogy by covering the period from 1930 through the Liberation, and is the narrative of the solidification, then crumbling apart of the Fascist regime, centered on the figure of an intellectual who clearly reflects the spiritual, intellectual, and moral experience of Pratolini himself. The historical element of this trilogy has impressed readers as the least successful, vitiating Pratolini's undeniable talent for character creation, particularly of working-class types. In moving out of the tight little proletarian world of a certain section of Florence to take on the broader canvass of historical and political events, Pratolini has dispersed the atmosphere of warm human affections and solidarity, and weakened that sense of intimacy with the poor and the wretched attained in his undoubted masterpiece, *Cronache di poveri amanti*. Readers have sensed, at least in the first two books of *Una storia italiana*, the cold quality which comes from the author's excessive fidelity to a thesis, and at least one caustic critic has suggested that with the trilogy Pratolini has moved from social realism to socialist realism. This barb is probably excessive, but there seems to be fairly general agreement that in moving away from his own kind of neorealism toward the political-historical novel Pratolini had achieved only a limited success.

Pratolini's change from chronicle to history is symptomatic of the crisis of neorealism apparent in the early and mid-1950's. It appears now that we can even speak of the death of the neorealistic "school" at that time, at least of that attitude toward fiction insisting on its direct social and sociological concern. Italian criticism in its evaluation of the novel since the mid-1950's has had trouble finding labels to identify the fiction being produced. Italy has had no existentialist school, no *nouveau roman, anti-roman* or *école du regard*. Instead of breaking dramatically with neorealism, the novel often has used the neorealist base as a point of departure for new directions in fiction. These directions do not, however, lead contemporary writing away from the humanistic concern which has been noted as one of its fundamental characteristics, an emphasis imparted to it by the two writers who were its moral guides, Pavese and Vittorini. With Vittorini's death in 1967 we have a further thinning of the ranks of the "second generation" figures. Pavese, it will be recalled, committed suicide in 1950. Both were very instrumental in the renewal of the Italian literary language, one of the outstanding accomplishments of their generation; and both served as innovators, theoreticians, rallying points, and critics who fulfilled an inspirational function, particularly for many younger writers. Perhaps these activities and preoccupations account for the fact that neither contributed a novel of compelling international stature to Italian literature. Pavese came closer than Vittorini to doing so in *La luna e i falò* (1950; *The Moon and the Bonfires,* 1952), a persuasive lyrical treatment of a theme with an appeal to many novelists of the second generation: the return of the wanderer to his native region after a long absence, as part of a search for identity. In this last novel Pavese achieved the most satisfactory balance of the individual and the collective, a goal he had constantly set for himself in his fiction. The search to find himself and the essential significance of his life leads the narrator, Anguilla, to engage in the seeming paradox of self-obliteration, as he attempts to understand the people, objects, and events of his childhood and youth, thus reducing his own life to an accessory role in the narrative. Eventually Anguilla departs from the scene just as unobtrusively as he had returned home, his brief visit having clarified the continuing strength of his bond with his native Piedmontese mountains, a bond which will exist wherever he goes. Although his friend Nuto's destiny was to stay, Anguilla had to experience the life of the outside world in order to overcome the particular stigma of his bastard origin and to prove himself. But his return brings understanding and acquiescence to what he realizes is his destiny, an indestructible spiritual identification with his own people and with the natural forces which have shaped them.

The theme of the "return" utilized so successfully by Pavese in *La luna e i falò* is one consequence of his fresh approach to realism in fiction. A novelist could not perceive or express reality, Pavese felt, without employing the device of memory, since our experiences can be fully understood only when we have relived them through memory. The most effective aid to this recall is a reimmersion in the physical atmosphere of the past. Regardless of their surroundings, however, his protagonists through the device of memory take their spiritual bearings in the present. Like Proust, Pavese viewed time as destructive of the unity life can offer, and the process of memory functions in his novels to minimize the sense of time, enveloping his world in an aura of timelessness. Pavese's journal records his agreement with the critic Georgy Lukacs that the twentieth-century novelist prefers to stress the changelessness of his "heroes," rather than their growth and development, which was the primary interest of the nineteenth-century novelist. *La luna e i falò* best illustrates this static relationship to time, in its concurrent unfolding on two time levels, that of reminiscence and memory and that of an immediate past, mutually enriching and closely interwoven. The level of memory dominates, as Anguilla makes himself the center of a spontaneous, unsequential series of remembrances, emanating from him in ever widening, concentric ripples. These thoughts, impressions, and comments reach out finally to enclose and clarify the destinies of the inhabitants of his native region. Even the more linear, direct narrative level, represented by the story of the lame peasant boy, Cinto, contributes to the circular design by suggesting in the strong similarities between him and Anguilla, the repetitive quality of life. The latter returns to his Piedmont to find that in the midst of great changes nothing essential has changed, and he is particularly struck by the realization that men live with the same myths which their ancestors accepted.[8]

Elio Vittorini, too, employed the theme of the "return" in his most successful work of fiction, *Conversazione in Sicilia,* an allegory or poetic fable whose wealth of imagery and myth enfolds too intricately and tightly the sense of human solidarity which inspired its author. The theme is used here symbolically to signify the necessity for a return to our common humanity, to primary values, to a sense of the dignity of life in simple provincial surroundings, a motif with a strong appeal to other novelists of this period.[9] Vittorini produced no subsequent fiction with the stature of *Conversazione in Sicilia.* This masterpiece has come to exemplify the innovation in technique and form of Italian fiction, attributable to him: a new priority of the intuitive and lyrical in the structure of narrative, reinforced by an epic thrust, in addition to a minimization of traditional intellective structure and plot line. Coloring the foregoing we find a profound and somewhat anguished humanitarian and humanistic concern with a dolorous "offended world" where the most human are the exploited poor. This populist quality in Vittorini is not to be found in Pavese whose lyricism is attained primarily through an emphasis on relived and reconsidered memories and myths of childhood and adolescence, as well as a mythically conceived opposition of city and countryside, which in Pavese's case meant Turin and the Piedmontese hills and mountains. The best fiction of Pavese and Vittorini is poetic through lyric, mythic, and symbolic devices, but Pavese's mood is more personal, reflecting his private anguish and suffering, his fundamental inability to come to terms with society and life, while Vittorini's sense of a suffering humanity seems conditioned by a more optimistic outlook.

Pavese, Vittorini, Pratolini, neorealism are important names and terms one must deal with in examining the literature of the early postwar period in Italian fiction. To these must be added that of today's best known Italian literary figure both in and outside of Italy, Alberto Moravia, who continues a literary career begun in 1927 with the appearance of *Gli indifferenti* (*The Indifferent Ones*, 1932; a superior translation appeared as *The Time of Indifference*, 1953). Moravia has now published almost a score of novels and novellas, several collections of short stories in addition to two plays, and is a prolific essayist, polemicist, and critic of literature, cinema, and general culture. As noted earlier, Moravia has been classified by some as a neorealist and the study of the contemporary Italian novel by the Frenchman Ramon Fernandez confirmed this view by examining his work from a pointedly neo-Marxist base.[10] A great deal of critical emphasis, in accordance with this interpretation, has been placed on the fiction of the Roman novelist as centrally concerned with the moral and spiritual degeneracy of the Italian middle class. While it is certainly valid to study Moravia's fiction from a Marxist viewpoint (he has somewhere stated that no contemporary novelist can afford to ignore Marx and Freud), the writer's moralistic concern with the state of the Italian bourgeoisie seems less important than his existential concern with the loneliness, boredom, and alienation of key characters in his works. Moravia's "neorealism" then must be said to conflict with his undeniably strong strain of existentialism. Complicating all this is an ability to vary mood and theme so that a very successful work such as *La Ciociara* (1957; *Two Women*, 1958) can be described as somewhat neorealistic because of its setting, characters, subject, and a certain socio-political idealism represented by its most important male character, whereas Moravia's next novel, *La Noia* (1960; *The Empty Canvas*, 1961) represents a return to his philosophical, almost Sartrean, emphasis.

The collections of short stories utilizing as a kind of core theme the "human comedy" of the Roman proletariat and lower middle classes which Moravia has continued to publish regularly in the postwar years illustrate once more his lack of interest in the early postwar brand of documentary neorealism since the suffering and misery of his lower-class characters is not permitted to override the narrator's primary concern with their irony-laden, often grotesque and tragicomic ways of reacting to their "human condition." Moravia's most recent novel, *L'attenzione*, (1965; *The Lie*, 1966) is the first of his fictional works to have abandoned almost completely the creation of characters set against some kind of a "realistic" background. In the form of a diary kept by the narrator-novelist who is its central personage, the unfolding novel itself is the protagonist of this work because it fulfills the primary function set by Moravia as the touchstone of truth. Here he has undertaken a Pirandellian examination of truth, sincerity, genuineness as they relate to reality. The basic philosophical assumption is the bewilderment of modern man as he attempts to grasp some kind of moral certainty and fails. For Francesco Merighi, the protagonist-narrator-diarist of *L'attenzione,* only the novel he is preparing to write can provide some kind of anchor, a certainty based on art, in a world of corruption and insincerity. Through Merighi, Moravia insists that evil has become normality and that this can unhinge the intelligent man who seeks to adhere to "normal" standards and values. Insofar as Moravia emphasizes the powerful elements of alienation in his three principal characters—Merighi, his estranged wife Cora, and his stepdaughter Baba—this latest novel can be termed existential. Unfortunately none of them arouse any real empathy in the reader, as they never really come to life behind the kind of haze in which the author envelops them. Moravia plays with his reader most disconcertingly here, since Merighi offers us factual reality and his own inventions in the diary, giving equal validity to both. And the dialogues retain the kind of woodenness for which Moravia is well-known in his less successful works, which we suppose is to be read as expressive of the woodenness of human relationships in today's world. *L'attenzione* does not seem destined to arouse in critics and readers the enthusiasm manifested on the appearance of *La Ciociara,* his most human, therefore his most optimistic work of fiction. Somehow this latest book is vitiated by excessive intellectuality and its esthetic-philosophical orientation. One should note, finally, that for better or for worse it is strikingly free of Moravia's usual concern with and presentation of sexuality.

The failure of critical attempts to link Moravia with any markedly strong current in contemporary Italian fiction can help us sense the measure of his singularity, while his existentialism—expressed discreetly, without intense or profound philosophical overtones—gives evidence of the selectivity he has exercised in studying the lessons of Pirandello. In notable contrast to the wider, more extensive canvas utilized by his contemporaries of the second generation, Moravia has chosen to portray a limited area of human experience. Thus he has been able to achieve an intensity in sharp contra-distinction to the loose, thin quality of many novels by his colleagues. This intensity makes possible the evoca-tion of mood, another quality often lacking in contem-porary Italian writing. In the attention he has contin-ued to pay such matters as plot and character (except in his latest novel) Moravia reveals himself as some-thing of a traditionalist, occupying, as Ramon Fernan-dez has stated, an intermediate position between the nineteenth-century novel and that of Joyce, Kafka, and Proust.

Much of the fiction of this second generation has taken another direction as far as the concept of charac-ter is concerned, a direction suggested by the three great writers just mentioned, and exemplified clearly by Pavese whose fascination with myth and the repeti-tiveness of all human experience caused him to adopt a dispersive theory of character. The reader who at-tempts to isolate personages as focal points for recall of numerous novels by writers of the second genera-tion will appreciate the validity of the comment. One reason why Giuseppe Tomasi di Lampedusa's evoca-tive historical recreation of post-Risorgimento Sicily, *Il Gattopardo* (1958; *The Leopard*, 1960) received such enthusiastic acclaim is because it returned una-shamedly to the nineteenth century for its concept of character.

Moravia's protagonists are nineteenth-century in their clear identity and in their psychological solidity, but modern in their vaguely explained sense of soli-tude. The depth of his pessimism can be gauged in our realization that his principal characters—with notably successful exceptions such as Agostino in the short novel of that title (1945; included in *Two Adoles-cents*, 1950), and Adriana, the prostitute-heroine of *La romana* (1947; *The Woman of Rome*, 1949)—are unable even to attempt to emerge from their psycho-logical limbo toward a sense of communion and companionship with others; or it might be said that this attempt is made on only one level—sex—and that it is not successful. Alienation then is the fundamental theme of Moravia's longer fiction, and it is only to that extent that he can be considered interested in man's relationship to society. While this statement does not deny the validity of the Marxist-oriented interpretation of Moravia's fiction as seeking to unmask the hypocrisy about sex which controls human relations in bourgeois and neo-capitalistic society, it puts the emphasis where it rightfully belongs, on the primary value and concern of Moravia's novels as moral and psychological, rather than social.

The fiction of Moravia is the most effective and best known example of the powerful current of sexuality characterizing a great deal of the writing of the postwar period. The near ancestor responsible for this orientation in Italian literature is Gabriele d'Annunzio. In sharp contrast to d'Annunzio's glorification of sexual freedom, Moravia ironically uses sexuality to imprison his characters in a web of intellectual impotence and sterility. Sex is often a dispiriting, degrading means by which the Moravian personage tries to assert an intellectual or moral force he does not possess, while sexuality takes on an unnaturalness and a quality of perversity numerous readers find somewhat shocking. Moravia's contemporary (and friend) the Catanian Vitaliano Brancati was also in reaction to d'Annunzian sexuality; indeed all the writing of his mature period (from 1935 until his death in 1954) is flavored by this retreat from his own early d'Annunzianism. Brancati, however, chose to satirize erotic excess on its traditional home grounds, the island of Sicily, as part of a more general comic critique of bourgeois and upper-class culture. His approach to sex, conditioned by traditional, even classical considerations, depends on the implicit presence of a healthy, natural norm of sexuality. If Moravia's characters are helpless victims of sensuality, then the times in which they live are primarily responsible. For Brancati, on the other hand, three factors—influence of ancestry, milieu, the times—are involved in the excessive sexuality of his personages, although of the three he is least concerned with the times. Exaggerated eroticism is an inheritance of Sicilian blood and the island's moral tradition; yet it is that environment which somehow prevents the denaturing and vitiation of his fictive world.

Through Brancati's imaginative re-creation of the erotic atmosphere of Eastern Sicily, and particularly of the bourgeois milieu to which he was born, in the early years of the present century to the 1950's we are clearly a long way from the Sicilians of Verga's and Pirandello's fiction. The selection of the bourgeoisie and the upper classes was significant, for Brancati's satire of eroticism does not deal with elemental, primitive passions. He is engrossed in the manners and morals of the Sicilian classes which are out of the struggle for mere material existence—from the small merchants and professional men through the land-owning nobility—choosing to satirize those in whom education and breeding have driven a wedge between sentiments and the senses, those who have uncritically accepted their heritage of erotic preoccupation, or who are unable to resist it effectively. Paradoxically Brancati has been classified as a Sicilian writer par excellence, the satirist of a characteristic Sicilian phenomenon, *gallismo*, when a closer acquaintance with his work and thought reveals him as one of the most European of Italian writers. His Europeanism was late-blooming, and came with a kind of desperate intensity after the deep spiritual and moral crisis from which he emerged in 1935, permanently scarred but purged of his enthusiasm for Fascism. The wider intellectual outlook Brancati sought to develop after 1935 was the natural reaction to his awareness of the limitations of his provincialism, the remedy for which he eventually convinced himself lay in rejoining the mainstream of European, rather than strictly Italian literature and culture. This solution was more than just a personal one; in Brancati's view it was the only way Italian culture could renew itself after being rendered sterile by Fascism. Later a number of his detractors failed to appreciate the connection he had established between his personal problem as an artist and the general situation of the arts and the life of the intellect in Fascist and post-Fascist Italy. They could not understand what lay behind the regular references in his writing, some more, some less direct, to his youthful Fascist errors. Contrary to their accusations, the Sicilian novelist was not indulging in masochistic breast-beating, but was perfectly sincere in his self-criticism, the purpose of which was to provide a salutary lesson to readers of his own and future generations.

As a corollary to his role as a "witness" of the spiritual and moral failings of Italy under Fascism and in the immediate postwar years, Brancati believed passionately in the role of the Italian writer as a goad to and as a voice of the Italian moral conscience. In the disinclination of the Italian people to examine their society critically and honestly he saw his country's most fundamental and serious defect. After 1935 and under the nose of the Fascist censorship he sought courageously to awaken the Italian conscience to the spiritual corruption of the regime and to the intellectual and philosophic dishonesty upon which it was based. His attacks, surprisingly direct at times, were in the form of essays and articles published in newspapers and reviews, in prefaces to books which he edited, and in his own short stories and novels. That he was able to avoid censorship and even imprisonment is testimony to both the obtuseness and the tolerance of the Fascist guardians of the press. The bitter lesson he learned after the fall of Mussolini was that the Italians' newly regained political liberty was not accompanied by a capacity or even a strong desire for critical self-examination. Brancati revealed his fundamental optimism (a quality too many of his critics failed to appreciate or understand) by challenging this defect of Italian culture, and continuing even more energetically and courageously in his postwar writing to pursue his comic, often satiric portrayal of Italian society and social types. This continuing moral passion produced its fruits in works like *Il vecchio con gli stivali* (*The Old Man With the Boots*), a long novella written and first published in 1945, which seems destined to remain one of the most sublimely comic commentaries on the Fascist experience ever written.

Briefly, its main theme is the ironic trick played by fate on a basically good but milktoastish southern Italian, forced by life to stifle his innate, commonsense antipathy to the Fascist regime, yet compelled tragically to suffer—after Italy was "liberated"—for having worn the black shirt and boots he detested. In the tragicomic story of Aldo Piscitello, Brancati managed to symbolize the whole experience of Italy under Fascism. The novelist's previous critique of the boredom and stupidities of Italian life under Mussolini was augmented by his biting but affectionate ironies on postwar human behavior. Brancati's lucid and ironic intelligence continued to probe the weaknesses of Italian society in a comic-serious vein in the novel *Il bell'Antonio* (1949; *Antonio, the Great Lover*, 1952), where he achieved his first successful fusion of the theme of exaggerated Sicilian eroticism (gallismo) with a satirical, sometimes caricatural portrait of Sicilian bourgeois society under Fascism. The six most significant comedies of the Catanian writer, plays whose themes largely echo those of his novels and short stories, were written in the postwar period. The fact that Brancati found it impossible to have them staged was due, in part at least, to a reluctance in official circles to permit such a direct mirror to be held up before the face of Italian society. In his last novel, *Paolo il caldo* (1955), unfinished at the time of his death and published posthumously, Brancati dimin-

ished the comic emphasis to underline a more tragic
vision of life, although in many respects the work can
be considered an updated, postwar society-centered *Il
bell'Antonio*. It offers a devastating caricature of artistic and intellectual society in Rome which most readers find largely unsuccessful, but which was clearly
inspired by the burning thirst for sincerity and truth
which characterizes Brancati's thought and its literary
expression.[11]

Despite Brancati's European outlook and his somewhat "unfashionable" stylistic (at least to Pavese-Vit-
torini oriented criticism) nineteenth-century approach
to the novel, he has been included in that somewhat
amorphous grouping of writers who have used as thematic material the social, economic, and political conditions of the Italian South. The fact that Carlo Levi,
Elio Vittorini, Ignazio Silone, among numerous others have been put into this category is indicative of the
diversity of approach to this "Southern" literature,
which owes so much to the two Sicilians Giovanni
Verga and Luigi Pirandello. The best qualities of neorealism, a passionate concern for a suffering humanity,
particularly as it is reflected in the lives of the lower
classes, the delineation of the rapport between the
peasant and the natural forces with which he must
deal (or between the lower classes and the state) the
examination of the disastrous moral and spiritual effects of war and injustice—all these are and have been
implicit or explicit characteristics of "Southern" literature since the last quarter of the nineteenth century. A
strong case could be made to support the assertion
that the modern and particularly the contemporary
novel in Italy has been shaped and influenced most
importantly by the so-called problem of the South.

A writer who particularly well represents a line of
continuity between the Verga tradition in Southern
fiction and present-day narrative, and who has affinities with Vittorini and Brancati, is Corrado Alvaro, a
member of the second generation, who died in 1956.

Alvaro offers one of the best examples of the successful blending of regionalistic and provincial thematic
material with the more cosmopolitan, "modern"
themes of European literature which was noted above
as a distinguishing characteristic of the best Italian
writing in the contemporary period. Thus he has been
labeled a "Southern" writer, the most notable and
distinguished recorder of Calabrian society, manners,
and landscape. Such a description of Alvaro contains
the same limitations of truth inherent in the statement that Verga was the outstanding interpreter and
portraitist of Sicilian life. As in the case of the Catanian master of "verismo," Alvaro uses his regionalistic
material as a basis for presenting and treating themes
and motifs of universal interest and importance.
While we can detect lessons learned from him by
novelists out of the neorealistic current such as Brancati and Moravia, it would be possible, to show defi-
nite signs of Alvaro's influence on Pavese, Vittorini,
Levi and on their neorealist successors.

Born in 1895, Alvaro came to maturity in the *prosa
d'arte* period of the Rondisti, a significant factor in the
development of his narrative style, whose complexity
and richness mitigate forcefully against what we might
call his thematic tendencies toward neorealism. Alvaro
and Vittorini have in common a lyrical approach to
the depiction of reality, a predilection for the fable
and fabulous as instruments for the evocation of atmosphere, and a compassion for a suffering humanity.
Alvaro, however, remains closer to his undoubted master, Verga, in his lack of a direct sense of *engagement*,
in emphasizing the inexorableness of a cruel destiny
shaping the lives of his characters, in his predilection
for a massive sense of irony to clarify men's struggles
against the facts of the human condition. *Gente in
Aspromonte* (1930; partially translated as *Revolt in
Aspromonte*, 1962) best exemplifies the qualities of
Alvaro's fiction just noted and its date of publication
confirms the need to include certain key works of the

prewar period in listings of contemporary literature. *L'uomo è forte* (1938; *Man is Strong*), which reflects Alvaro's early (during the twenties) and continuing anti-Fascism reveals his predilection for psychological analysis that is applied in this case to a somewhat Kafkaesque study of the mind and soul of man suffering under totalitarian dictatorship. Two factors contribute to the failure of this novel, otherwise so significant as a work of protest: a lack of realism in its character portraits and an overpresence of its thesis.

Alvaro's pre-World War II literary career, in addition to his regular activity as a journalist, was reflected in a dozen volumes of narrative fiction, ten books of essay and travel writings, three volumes of poetry, two plays and a number of translations from English, Russian, and Greek writers. After 1946 his activity was divided between the essay-diary and fiction, in a focus very much like that of Brancati, so akin to Alvaro in his passionate moral and ethical concern. Both of these Southern-oriented writers in important respects remain outside the main stream of postwar Italian literature in spite of the fact that their activity continued forcefully until the mid-1950's. They were formed by a cultural and literary tradition more nineteenth-century or more pre-World War I than that which shaped the Paveses and the Vittorinis (although Brancati belonged chronologically with the latter). While it is true that Vittorini reveals a great admiration for Stendhal, it is in Brancati's and Alvaro's fiction and essay-diary writings that the Stendhalian flavor and stylistic echo are often to be detected. (The same is true for the narrative fiction of the author of *Il Gattopardo*, Tomasi di Lampedusa.) Alvaro takes his place with Brancati, in the best Stendhalian tradition, as a keenly analytical observer and witness of contemporary Italian society, desperately aware of its failings and shortcomings as a reflection of inadequacies and weaknesses in the national character. In addition to the two volumes of journal-essay writings, *Quasi una vita, giornale d'uno scrittore* (1950; *Almost a Life: Journal of a Writer*) and *Ultimo diario* (*Final Diary*), published posthumously in 1959,[12] Alvaro composed a trilogy in the postwar period consisting of *L'età breve* (1946), and two books published posthumously, *Mastrangelina* (1960) and *Tutto è accaduto* (1961). These three novels, of which only the first was published in its finished form, comprise a social and moral inquiry into Italian bourgeois society first under Fascism, then in the years after World War II. Their emphasis is on two themes which have attracted the attention of a number of contemporary, particularly Southern novelists: the sexual education of the young men of the South, as it is affected by the interplay of mutually antagonistic forces, a repressive moralistic tradition set against the need for a virility conceived in terms of *gallismo*; and the problem posed for young Southerners particularly by the social phenomenon of rapidly increasing urbanization and continuing movement from the rural areas to the cities.

Unlike Brancati who employed a comic approach to his depiction of Italian morals and manners, Alvaro created a fictional world full of dramatic tensions, incipient violence colored by a dominant seriousness and gravity of tone and atmosphere. Neither Alvaro nor Brancati has enjoyed more than a grudging acceptance by Marxist-oriented literary criticism in Italy. In explanation we may suggest two principal reasons: first, their fiction avoids the spirit of existential engagement in the more direct politically and sociologically polemical manner. Another way to put this is to state that, in spite of their perceptiveness and lucidity as observers of manners and morals of modern Italian society, they have no ideological solutions to propose to reform it, even implicitly. The second factor in this critical reserve is their preference for a more richly textured, imagistic, at times baroque, style which owes much to Flaubert and the nineteenth-century novel tradition, and which seems unfashionable when com-

pared with the linearity, directness, and stylistic bareness which Pavese and Vittorini brought into Italian
fiction.

The observations, information, and summaries given
have sought to clarify both the general significance of
literary neorealism for the newer Italian narrative and
to indicate some of the writers and areas where its
influence was not so direct. An attempt must now be
made to identify some significant trends in Italian
fiction since the crisis of neorealism, and to discuss a
few of the outstanding newer or newly appreciated
novelists.

There is little disagreement among critics of recent
Italian narrative literature that since the mid-1950's
published works have reflected the increasing distance
from the war and its destructive immediate aftermath.
The sharpness of certain ideological positions, based
on the Resistance and the civil war, has become sof-
tened, as developments in the social, economic, and
political situation of Italy and other parts of Europe
enriched the perspective of the novelist. One might
mention as a case in point the disillusionment of the
Marxist intellectuals in Italy as a result of the Russian
repression of the Hungarian uprising in 1956. Many
Italian writers abandoned the extreme Left as a result.
On the other hand the buffeting of the idealism generated by the downfall of the Fascist regime upon the
return, after the De Gasperi governments, to a kind of
cynical politics-as-usual by the controlling Christian
Democratic Party confirmed some writers in their
moderate Leftist, if not Communist positions. One
must not make too much of this ideological problem,
of course, since it is important to reiterate that there
has been relatively little direct intrusion of politics and
political polemic in Italian narrative fiction. Yet it
seems fair to state that the situation in Italy since
about 1955 has encouraged many novelists to examine

the recent past with a more balanced, impartial attitude than was possible in the immediate postwar
years.

The added perspective on recent history has been
beneficial to the novelist, as he has sought to analyze,
clarify, recreate the spirit and the qualities of life during the prewar period especially. Italo Calvino has
described this trend or current in recent Italian narrative as "the replacement of the epic with the elegy,
which involves the exploration of sentiment and psychology in a melancholy mood."[13] The epic he refers
to would be the literature of the Resistance and the
War. Calvino sees the development as a traditional
one in Italian writing, commenting that "every time
action dies out, literature has retreated from epic to
elegy."[14] The most extreme example one can cite in
support of Calvino's suggestion is the case of Giuseppe
Tomasi di Lampedusa's *Il Gattopardo* mentioned earlier. A historical novel in its evocation of Garibaldian
and post-Garibaldian Sicily, the most strikingly successful quality of Lampedusa's work lies in the affec-
tionately ironical—yet almost nostalgic—recreation of
a world inevitably doomed by history and its own
defects to bow to bourgeois "progress." It is a world
whose passing in some ways saddens the heart. Elegiac
elements in the narrative works of Carlo Levi, Corrado Alvaro, Vasco Pratolini could be pointed out
also, but this tendency in recent literature has been
most successfully illustrated by two highly esteemed
figures of the contemporary novel, Carlo Cassola and
Giorgio Bassani.

Cassola's first published fiction, mostly narrative
sketches and short stories, dates from the early 1940's
and his developing literary career brought him to the
longer form of the novel in 1952 with the appearance
of *Fausto e Anna* (*Fausto and Anna*, 1960). Since
then he has published close to ten volumes of fiction
(including a revised edition of *Fausto e Anna*) and
been acclaimed one of the leading stylists on the con-

temporary scene. His *La ragazza di Bubé* (1960; *Bébo's Girl*, 1962) was awarded the Strega literary prize. Two novellas *Il Taglio del bosco* (1954) and *Il Soldato* (1958) additionally have been important in establishing his reputation. For Cassola the War and particularly the Resistance movement was crucial in his human and literary maturation. It confirmed and strengthened in him a pre-existing tendency, seen in his early short fiction, to prefer narrative centered on the sentimental, social, and political education of sensitive, gentle people, characters too easily wounded in their struggles with a harsh, unfeeling world, but who become strengthened in the course of their often pathetic conflict. It is a paradox that this compassionate attitude, fundamental to Cassola's fictional world, is expressed in a style by now renowned in Italy for its impersonality, essentiality, bareness, and brevity.

Fausto e Anna is a good example of the blending of epic and elegiac atmospheres, and especially the more dispassionate and esthetically distanced treatment of the War and the Resistance characteristic of Cassola, Bassani and other Italian novelists of the 1950's and 1960's. Set in the towns and countryside of the Tuscan Maremma region where Cassola was born and raised, it is the novel of a generation, presenting the ambitions, hopes, frustrations, and failures of provincial youth from the early thirties through World War II. While the disillusionment and vitiation of youth is a commoner theme among contemporary novelists, in Italy and elsewhere, than innocence, *Fausto e Anna*, in spite of its elegiac sadness, is permeated with a freshness and unsophistication heightened by the implicit contrast with a society in ferment. Symbolic and significant is the limited, accessory role of the older generations which lack the vitality to arouse resistance and revolt. Cassola's young people must find their way to maturity unaided. Perhaps what I call their innocence should be termed a total lack of cynicism, evidenced in a simplicity and directness of response to life, reminding one often of the great Russian writers. Cassola's fiction eschews the superficial and accidental in life to concentrate on essence. He distills experience into poetry without literary pretense, by means of a sparseness, immediacy, incisiveness of style capable of deceiving the careless or unalert reader.

Fausto e Anna is the narrative of an *éducation sentimentale,* its protagonist is something of an *artiste manqué.* While it has some Flaubertian overtones, it lacks irony, the indispensable element in post-Romantic sensibility. Another important difference is the slenderness and unpretentiousness of the presentation, reflecting the extraordinary reserve and essential humility of Cassola's artistic temperament. The Resistance theme gives this novel not only documentary significance but provides the background for the moral and sentimental growth of the hero, Fausto Errera, a young professor who joins the Partisans in the Tuscan mountains in 1944. The first half of the story recounts the adolescent loves of Fausto and Anna Mannoni, the pretty daughter of a minor provincial official, and it hardly prepares us for the change of direction and emphasis occurring in Part Two. A structural symmetry in the pattern of the story is revealed, however, as it unfolds. A futile striving for self-realization destroys Fausto's chance for happiness with Anna and furnishes the climax for the first part of the novel. The hero's Partisan experience, after Anna's marriage to a more typical young Italian, Miro, offers him finally the basis for coming to terms with life, the self-confidence he has always needed. The novel's discreet and perhaps solitary irony is the resurgence of Fausto and Anna's love for each other, with its seemingly illimitable promise, doomed despite the brief idyllic happiness the swelling tide of the Resistance movement offers them.

Unlike many of the neorealist writers in the decade after the war who utilized the Resistance theme, Cassola attempted no ideologically inspired idealization.

Of the "political" aspect of this work he utilized only what contributed to the development of his protagonist. Fausto joined the Partisans not because of political moral idealism, but because he felt the necessity of participation to satisfy a personal, rather than social need. His political innocence (he was the only non-Communist or non-Socialist in the band) developed, with the broadening of his experience and knowledge of men, into a rejection of partisanship and politics. He emerged from the Resistance movement with a distrust of systems and any form of dogmatism, reinforced in his generous humanity and his hatred of man's violence to the dignity of other men. The sense of human solidarity and brotherhood he gained from his participation in the Partisan warfare successfully counterbalanced for Fausto its bloodshed, violence, and cruelty. This admittedly tenuous affirmative note in the portrait of Fausto is not paralleled in that of Anna, whose destiny more effectively exemplifies the fundamental sadness of Cassola's fiction. Her provincial girlhood which alternately provided simple joys and solitary boredom terminated with the necessity for making difficult choices. Marriage with the charming but egotistical Miro left her hungering for a sense of identity and spiritual fulfillment, satisfactions possible with the mature, but now unattainable Fausto.

Cassola's Strega prize winning novel *La ragazza di Bubé* best supports a statement by Italo Calvino pointing to a recurrent theme in both Cassola's and Giorgio Bassani's fiction: "the melancholy of a provincial life that has closed in again about existence after the great moment of truth represented by the Resistance." [15] This novel too is about an *éducation sentimentale*, but it has a heroine, rather than a hero. Mara belongs to a character type for whose artistic realization Cassola has achieved a justly deserved reputation, the young female incarnation of sense and sensibility in Italian provincial life. Mara's too is a pathos-filled story of unhappy love, in her case with a young ex-Partisan involved in a revenge murder, incited by the hatreds raised by the War. The principal narrative interest is in the sentimental and moral development of the heroine, whose growth from innocence and ingenuity through a series of tragic vicissitudes to inner fortitude, maturity, independence, and the capacity for self-sacrifice are unfolded by a sensitive, sympathetic, and compassionate narrator. Another novel, *Un cuore arido* (1961; *An Arid Heart*), further confirms Cassola's special competence in portraying the unsophisticated young woman of provincial Tuscany. This work which lacks the Resistance element, taking place in the years before World War II, focuses particularly on the solitude of provincial life for its heroine whose superiority to her surroundings earns her the ironic appellation of "the girl with the arid heart." Anna Cavorzio is no rebel; what her family and neighbors in her seaside village in the Tuscan Maremma consider aridity of heart is her honesty and reserve which protect her from the cant and hypocrisy, as well as the compromises and the masks, forced on individuals by society. Anna's story, as Cassola relates it, lacks sparkle and excitement, offering an elegiac, rather than dramatic or suspenseful quality. But he succeeds almost immediately in persuading the reader that most important in Anna's story are not its events but the atmosphere, the tone, and the rhythm of her existence. Like Mara (and other heroines and heroes in Cassola's stories), Anna learns to accept her destiny of solitude with courage and resignation.

Cassola's stylistic reserve, the deliberate emphasis on the minor and marginal aspects of reality, his reduction of the observer's scope, and his filtering out of all but the most essential elements of things observed represent a distinctly original stylistic approach in contemporary Italian fiction and have earned him a solid position with the critics. Stylistically speaking Giorgio Bassani is far from Cassola, but he is often mentioned with the latter as an intimistic, autobiographical "crepuscular" narrator, with a strong lyrical and melancholic strain. There are certain other similarities: both offer a limited scope of regional experience, with Cassola concentrating on the Volterra area of Tuscany, while Bassani has been recognized as the chronicler of the city of Ferrara, and particularly of its Jewish community; both writers have utilized frequently the theme of solitude and of social, if not existential, alienation; and a common gravity and seriousness in their writing is rarely, if ever, disturbed by a comic or light-hearted note; finally both writers were slow in attempting the longer form of the novel, serving a kind of apprenticeship first in the shorter forms of fiction. Bassani is perhaps the most atmospheric and evocative of present-day Italian novelists, and it is thus hardly surprising to learn that he was responsible for the "discovery" of Tomasi di Lampedusa's *Il gattopardo* while an editor of the Feltrinelli publishing house. His richly textured, imagistic style is enriched by a superb visual memory. Objects, rooms, houses, streets are endowed with the life of the characters who people them; a time spirit is magically recreated but the chronicle quality, as in the best work of Pratolini, is constantly transformed into poetry. Ferrara is a provincial city and its Jewish community might seem to offer a restricted area of experience for the scope of the modern novel. Bassani succeeds in recreating the particular flavor of that special world and at the same time persuades us how crucial its fate has been in the larger picture of our recent moral and spiritual history. He is able to do this primarily because, although a Jew, he is unmistakably an Italian writer (just as Bernard Malamud is an American, not a Jewish novelist). One cannot help being reminded of Proust, reading this evocative history of the Ferrara Jewish community from the 1920's through its catastrophic destruction during the war. For one who has fully participated in that history, Bassani maintains a rare objectivity and sense of perspective. There is nostalgia

and affection in his bittersweet memories of the en-
closed, protective middle-class world of his childhood
and youth, a world full of books, friends, school, family,
sports, Adriatic-beach summers. But there is also an
awareness of the threats to comfortable middle-class
values, an appreciation of the instability of human
relationships, a subtle skill in the expressing with
poetic reserve the unpredictable and the mysterious
aspects of personality and behavior.

Bassani's best known fiction works are the *Cinque
storie ferraresi* (1956; *Five Tales of Ferrara*), *Gli oc-
chiali d'oro* (1958; *The Gold-Rimmed Spectacles*),
and his first long novel, *Il giardino dei Finzi-Contini*
(1962; *The Garden of the Finzi-Continis*). A new
expanded collection of the Ferrara stories appeared in
1960, and in 1964 was published *Dietro la porta*, an
autobiographical novelette of the author's schoolboy
years. While the *Storie ferraresi* were composed as
separate short stories and novellas they are unified by a
reappearance of characters from one work to another,
and, even more significantly, by their implicit function
as chapters in that chronicle of twentieth-century Ferrara, and particularly of its Jewish community. Unity
through a common point of view is furnished by the
presence of Bassani, who most often utilizes first person narration. *Il giardino dei Finzi-Contini* is unques-
tionably Bassani's most successful work up to now and
an excellent example of his singular qualities as a
narrator: his power of evoking atmosphere and endow-
ing it with a sense of mystery, of focusing a strange,
magical light on existence and the world. It is a love
story, simply and movingly told, with a minimum of
action, incident, suspense, or drama (like the stories of
Cassola) set in the late 1930's when the anti-Semitic
racial laws of the Mussolini regime suddenly came to
destroy the comfortable self-sufficiency of the Ferrara
Jews. Ironically this development was the occasion for
an opportunity long awaited by the retrospective narrator, an entrance into the closed world of the one

Jewish family which had remained aloof from its core-ligionists, the aristocratic, wealthy Finzi-Continis, possessors of a vast estate, with fabulous grounds and gardens, a superb private library, and a tennis court. The exclusion of the Ferrara Jews from the public tennis courts resulted in an invitation to the narrator to play on that of the Finzi-Continis, where he came to know the son Alberto and to fall in love with the daughter Micol. The major portion of the narrative describes with the most delicate psychological nuances the vagaries of this love, unrequited by Micol, who desires no more than friendship and who has a mysterious sense of the tragic destiny which awaits her entire family in the as yet unheard of death camps of Nazi Germany. *Il Giardino* is Bassani's "remembrance of things past" and, although focused on only a fraction of the reality he experienced, it somehow expands to encompass, with fragile tenderness of recollection, a time and a world which Bassani has rendered pathetically unforgettable. In reference to this work one critic has observed that Bassani "is one of the few contemporary novelists in Italy to have created believable characters who read, think, breathe, and live thoroughly the culture of their time." [16] Through the rich inner life he has given them, Bassani has demonstrated fidelity to an older esthetic of fiction. But his keen intelligence and analytic power are not restricted to the portraiture of introspectives. Taken together his personages truthfully suggest a time spirit, and the life of a provincial Italian city becomes a microcosm of the world.

The development of recent Italian fiction from neo-realism to autobiographically influenced elegiac memory is a significant but by no means dominant trend. Carlo Cassola is perhaps the most exemplary case in point; Giorgio Bassani's psychological subtleties and his richly textured style have no place in the neorealist esthetic, even though he has written a long short-story of convincing power on the Resistance theme "Una notte del '43" concerning a massacre of Partisans in the center of Ferrara instigated by a local Fascist official. Another type of development from neorealism can be seen in the fiction of Italo Calvino whose critical observations have been cited earlier in this essay. Calvino's growth as a narrator has been significantly influenced by both Pavese and Vittorini but his originality and independence are unquestioned, and he is considered one of the most promising of the third generation. (He was born in 1923.) His first significant work of fiction *Il sentiero dei nidi di ragno* (1947; *The Path to the Nest of Spiders*, 1957) revealed that Calvino was capable of more than just the documentary realism and the ideologically inspired adventure narrative of other Resistance fiction, full of blood, violence, and cruelty. Calvino demonstrated his artistic ingenuity by choosing to depict the civil war in Northern Italy from the viewpoint of an adolescent boy, Pin, who is caught up in the Partisan warfare which sweeps over his village and the surrounding mountains. The essential form of the narrative is in the subtle tension between the grave reality of historical events and a courageous boy's insistence on preserving the poetry, if not the innocence of childhood. Calvino has described the book "as a combination of *For Whom the Bell Tolls* and Robert Louis Stevenson." The fable quality of narrative atmosphere maintained by Calvino in this novella is his distinguishing characteristic as a story-teller and has been continued and developed in his short stories, *I Racconti* (1959) and especially in a trilogy of novels: *Il visconte dimezzato* (1952; *The Cloven Viscount*, 1962), *Il barone rampante* (1957; *The Baron in the Trees*, 1959), and *Il cavaliere inesistente* (1959; *The Non-existent Knight*, 1962).

A strong flavor of chivalric epic characterizes all three works of the trilogy which has been republished in one volume under the general title of *I nostri antenati* (1960) and it is hardly surprising to learn that

Calvino has an intense admiration for the Ferrarese Renaissance poet-narrator Ludovico Ariosto, author of the *Orlando furioso*. Like his master of the sixteenth century Calvino has sought to utilize a dominant spirit of adventurous fancy to vivify a narrative with a profound moral meaning. Like Ariosto, Calvino does not explicitly insist that his narrative be read within a strict ideological or moral frame of reference; he is content to permit the reader to make whatever interpretation he wishes; and it is indeed possible to read the trilogy without concerning oneself with its philosophical or moral intent. For the curious reader Calvino supplied an explanatory statement of the genesis of the three novels in the combined edition of 1960, a statement which throws light on the author's politico-ideological orientation as it developed from the end of his neorealistic period in the early 1950's to a more existentialist-tinged individualistic position.

Il visconte dimezzato, the most surrealistic of the three fantasies, is the tale of Medardo, an Italian nobleman split in half by a Turkish cannonball during the Thirty Years War, who survives as half a man to return to his domain. Unfortunately it is the evil half of his body and spirit which returns and the narrative in large part is the account, told by a young servant on the domain, of his nefarious deeds against all who come into contact with him, until the eventual surprising return on the scene of and reunification with his good half which had been carried away but not destroyed by the cannonball. Calvino makes use of a number of secondary characters and character groups to represent directly or indirectly certain types of contemporary man or certain attitudes which he depicts satirically or with gentle, delicate irony: the technician who is unable to make any ethical or moral connection between the ever more perfect inventions and machines for which he is responsible and the society which is to use them or be enslaved by them; the dispassionate, insensitive man of science who feels no bond with living humanity; the malady of estheticism and decadence which affect certain intellectual and artistic groupings; and the hypocritical moralism of the Protestant work ethic which claims religious values it does not in fact possess. The delicate and subtle satire is blended so discreetly with the plot elements that it is perfectly possible not to be struck by the ideological "message," Calvino's conviction that contemporary man must end his Marxian sense of alienation, overcome his Freudian sense of repression, recover his lost harmony and become a whole being again.

The moral-ideological "thesis" of *Il barone rampante* is somewhat easier to discern perhaps because of the exemplary role of the protagonist-hero of this tale, which bears strong resemblances to the *conte philosophique*. Cosimo di Rondò, a young Ligurian nobleman of independent spirit, is driven by parental repression and the tyranny of a sister to take refuge in a tree of the vast luxuriant forest which still covered the Italian Riviera region in the eighteenth century. Once aloft he decides never to return to earth, and the tale of his life, loves, and adventures in the trees is told by his sympathetic but rather puzzled younger brother. The underlying fantasy of the narrative is convincingly supported by the wealth of realistic, even historical detail, Calvino enthusiastically provides, more so in the case of this story than in the *Visconte dimezzato*. Cosimo abandons the earth, but not the life, the activity, the spirit of his times or of his fellow men. His full experience includes scientific investigation, participation in wars and revolutions, government, and an idyllic romance with an aristocratic young beauty who once lived nearby. At the end of his life he is carried off by a Montgolfier balloon which disappears over the sea.

Calvino has avowed a preference for telling stories about characters who set difficult goals for themselves in life and then work courageously and indefatigably to reach them as part of a search for integrity and wholeness of personality. Cosimo di Rondò is obviously the incarnation of that ideal and his harmonious "totality" can serve as a contrast to the alienated, repressed types of humanity presented in the story of the viscount Medardo. This theme of mutilation or alienation versus integrity and inner harmony is taken up again by Calvino in *Il cavaliere inesistente*. More Ariostesque than ever, Calvino sets this fable-like fantasy in the time of Charlemagne and presents as its central character a suit of armor which goes through all the motions of life but is empty inside. He enriches his story with all the trappings and atmosphere of medieval chivalry, including quests, warrior maidens, perilous journeys, and the vindication of knightly honor. Of the three novels this last, faithful to Ariosto, has the most tenuous link with everyday reality and correspondingly its imaginative fantasy is the most daring and captivating. Agilulfo, the nonexistent knight, symbolizes another defect of contemporary society; he is modern artificial man, an automaton, a part of objective reality who has lost all spiritual relationships with life, feels no bond with nature or history, and functions rationally as an abstraction. As an opposing figure to Agilulfo, Calvino creates his squire Gurdulù, the incarnation of totally sensual existence, conscienceless, who identifies completely with the irrational and earthly. The mechanism of the narrative is moved by a contrast or opposition of these two partial personages with two young knight-heroes Rambaldo and Torrismondo who represent two aspects of a search for identity and harmonious completeness; the former finds himself through the morality of action and experience, the latter through the pursuit of an absolute.

The three novels of *I nostri antenati* represent for Calvino three types of experience in self-realization, in the attainment of true spiritual liberty. The moral significance he has skillfully and delicately built into these tales blending fantasy and objective reality is hardly insistent and they offer simple narrative values with a direct, unintellectual fascination, and appeal. Calvino is an unsophisticated, unpretentious stylist with a gift of simplicity stemming from his deep interest in Italian fable literature. *I nostri antenati,* by successfully fusing lyric, epic, and comic elements with a discreet moral view of contemporary man, has provided a fresh viewpoint and technique to recent Italian fiction.

Among contemporary Italian novelists Carlo Emilio Gadda is the best known representative (along with Pier Paolo Pasolini) of what Calvino has called the fiction of linguistic tension. The term refers to narrative which has assigned an important function, both expressive and expressionistic, to the various regional dialects of Italy as well as to the various sub-languages, including slang, inevitably developed by a compartmentalized, specialized, and technological society. Gadda, now in his seventies, published his first book in 1931 and is probably the most respected and admired Italian writer by those engaged in the craft. His work has had an exemplary influence on the experimentalism attracting large numbers of younger novelists of the third generation in the last decade. Seminal in this new wave of Italian fiction was the publication in 1957 of Gadda's *Quer pasticciaccio brutto de via Merulana* (*That Awful Mess on Via Merulana,* 1965), a rambling, inconclusive detective story about a sordid crime in the Fascist Rome of the 1920's, transformed by Gadda into a caustically comic critique of contemporary life. The author uses a rich mixture of standard Italian, Roman dialect, Fascist officialese, and police and underworld argot in an extravagantly ebullient, often lyrical fashion, suggesting the linguistic vitalism of James Joyce, François Rabelais, and the Renaissance satirist Teofilo Folengo. His avant-garde role depends on stylistic innovations and particularly on a "liberation" of fiction from traditional rational structures even neorealism had been unable to avoid. Gadda has legitimized the mixture of amazingly diverse levels of cultural materials and linguistic strata in this composite style, alternating a built-up and release of tensions and energies labeled baroque by some critics. Masterfully controlling this technique is a corrosive intelligence working to unmask the tricksters and deceivers on every level of society, from the lowest underworld types to those in the highest places. Thus the police-novel aspect of *Quer pasticciaccio*, through a subtle use of stream-of-consciousness and inner-monologue devices, gives way constantly to observations and perceptions of moral-ideological character, often clothed in a bitter lyricism. The author's black humor regularly casts deflationary darts at the swollen phenomenon of Mussolini and Fascist turgidity, when it is not revealing, tongue-in-cheek fashion, the moral and ethical bankruptcy of the Italian middle classes. *La Cognizione del dolore* (1963), the basis for Gadda's award of the Fomentor International Literary Prize in that year, is a more accessible novel than *Quer pasticciaccio*, although it too depends heavily on dialectal and philological elements. It is a grotesque satire of Lombard society in the last years of Fascism, worked around an autobiographical portrait of the author, particularly underlining his desperate solitude. This statement of Gadda's own neurosis recounts the slothful life of Gonzalo Pirobuttino d'Eltino, a miser and a glutton, congenitally incapable of happiness, who lives an attraction-repulsion relationship with his aged mother, venerated, but also blamed by him for his infelicity because her bourgeois ideals of decorum have ruined his life. The story is set in an imagined South American country but the scene is recognizable as Gadda's Lombardy.

Gadda belongs to no literary school and he has retained a fierce artistic and social independence. He offers one of the most powerful expressions of the alienation and the sense of solitude which have increasingly attracted the newer Italian novelists as themes for fiction. His primary appeal to the third generation of narrators, in addition to a literary justification of neurosis, is a new approach to reality by means of linguistic and syntactical distortions and deformations, by dialect mixtures, verbal invention, and philological counterpoint. In addition, he has made neurosis fashionable as subject matter for the younger Italian novelists. This oeuvre, respected, if not popular or understood by the general Italian reader is, unfortunately, to the highest degree untranslatable. It is too early to assess the qualitative aspects of Gadda's influence on the Italian novel, but his literary image seems to be the most exciting one for the newer writers.

Notes

Soviet Russian Fiction BROWN

1. "Dva tovarishcha," *Novy Mir*, No. 1 (1967), p. 87. No translation of this work has yet been published in English. Other works in this category will henceforth be indicated as "NT" in the following notes.

2. Sinyavsky's fiction appears under the pseudonym Abram Tertz.

3. The transcript of the trial of Sinyavsky and his friend Yuli Daniel appears in Max Hayward (ed.), *On Trial: The Soviet State versus "Abram Tertz" and "Nikolai Arzhak,"* New York, 1966.

4. "Na Irtyshe," *Novy Mir*, No. 2 (1964), pp. 3–80. A translation appeared in *Soviet Literature*, No. 7 (1965), pp. 3–94.

5. "Dvoe," *Novy Mir*, No. 4 (1964), pp. 21–67 and 5 (1964), pp. 5–51. NT.

6. *Svidaniye s Nefertiti*, Moscow, 1965, pp. 204–5. NT.

7. *Ibid.*, pp. 409–10.

8. A. Adamovich, quoted in L. Lazarev, "Samoe velikoe dokazatel'stvo," *Novy Mir*, No. 11 (1966), p. 259.

9. M. Kuznetsov, "Kogda nachinaetsya novy period?" *Voprosy Literatury*, No. 7 (1964), p. 11.

10. "Semero v odnom dome," *Novy Mir*, No. 6 (1965), p. 75. NT.

11. "Apel'siny iz Morokko," *Yunost'*, No. 1 (1963), p. 4. NT.

12. The translation appears in Andrew R. Mac Andrew (tr.), *Four Soviet Masterpieces*, New York, 1965.

13. Also in *Four Soviet Masterpieces*.

14. L. Lazarev, "K Zvezdam," *Voprosy Literatury*, No. 9 (1961), p. 35.

15. *Takoe Dolgoe Detstvo*, Leningrad, 1965, pp. 8–10. NT.

16. *Ibid.*, pp. 179–80.

17. *Ibid.*, p. 205.

18. A. Kogan, "Geroi i vremya," *Voprosy Literatury*, No. 7 (1964), p. 37.

19. Aleksandr Borshchagovsky, "Poiski molodoi prozy," *Moskva*, No. 12 (1962), p. 207.

20. Anatoli Kuznetsov, "Kachestvo i eshche raz kachestvo," *Voprosy Literatury*, No. 12 (1961), p. 19.

21. "Literatura i yazyk," *Voprosy Literatury*, No. 6 (1967), p. 89. Aksenov suggested that this be attributed to the influence of Dostoevsky. In Stalin's time, Dostoevsky's influence was considered generally pernicious.

22. Lazarev, *op. cit.*, p. 35.

23. Igor' Motyashov, "Put' k rodnikam," *Moskva*, No. 1 (1966), p. 201.

24. Borshchagovsky, p. 209.

25. Ark. El'yashevich, "Nerushimoe edinstvo," *Zvezda*, No. 8 (1963), p. 198.

26. Lazarev, p. 28.

27. Borshchagovsky, p. 206.

28. Lazarev, p. 35.

29. V. Novikov, "Poeziya deistvitel'nosti," *Znamya*, No. 4 (1966), p. 218.

30. A. Marchenko, "Ispytaniye rabotoi," *Voprosy Literatury*, No. 12 (1961), p. 29.

31. Abram Tertz, "On Socialist Realism," in *The Trial Begins* and *On Socialist Realism*, New York, 1965.

The Italian Novel   TENENBAUM

1. "Main Currents in Italian Fiction Today," *Italian Quarterly*, IV, nos. 13–14 (Spring-Summer, 1960), p. 3.

2. Roberto Farinacci was a journalist and an early vociferous, indefatigable Fascist. He acted as a watchdog over the cultural scene and was appointed Minister of State in 1938.

3. Milan, Bompiani, p. 174.

4. The most thorough study of this subject is to be found in Donald Heiney's *America in Modern Italian Literature*. New Brunswick, Rutgers University Press, 1964.

5. Calvino, "Main Currents in Italian Fiction Today," p. 5.

6. Quoted in Vittorini's *Diario in pubblico*, Milano, Bompiani, 1957, p. 316. The translation is my own.

7. *Ibid.*, p. 316.

8. A more detailed discussion may be found in Louis Tenenbaum, "Character Treatment in Pavese's Fiction," *Symposium* (Summer 1961), pp. 131–38.

9. Ignazio Silone had made it a core motif in his *Vino e Pane* (1955; *Bread and Wine*, 1936) published during his exile in Switzerland in 1936. A spiritual, if not a physical return, is central to Carlo Levi's *Christ Stopped at Eboli*. Moravia's *La Ciociara* (1957; *Two Women*, 1958) centers on the return of its protagonist to her native region and the consequences of that sojourn in the rural region southeast of Rome.

10. *Le roman italien et la crise de la conscience européene.* Paris, Bernard Grasset, 1958.

11. Fuller treatment of Brancati is given by Louis Tenenbaum, "Vitaliano Brancati & Sicilian Eroticism," *Books Abroad*, XXXI, No. 3 (Summer, 1957), pp. 233–36, and "Vitaliano Brancati: 1907–1954," *Cesare Barbieri Courier*, VII, No. 1 (Fall, 1964), pp. 3–10.

12. *Ultimo diario* could very profitably be read with Brancati's *Diario romano* (1961) as direct testimony, by some of her most perceptive and intelligent minds, of life, politics, morals, and manners in Italy from 1927 to the mid-Fifties.

13. Calvino, p. 7.

14. *Ibid.*, p. 7.

15. *Ibid.*, p. 8.

16. Sergio Pacifici, "Italy 1962: Literary Trends and Books," *Cesare Barbieri Courier*, V., No.1 (Fall 1962), p. 9.

Index